Design for **Government**

Gensler

Gensler Publications
Two Harrison Street, Suite 400
San Francisco, CA 94105 USA

ISBN: 978-0-9826312-0-1

Library of Congress Control Number: 2010922395

Contents

Foreword

Government is more visible than ever today as the leader and crucial partner of initiatives that are vital to the diverse communities it serves. Whatever form government takes, effective performance is what it increasingly emphasizes. Government sees itself now as a benchmark, not just pushing for change, but also exemplifying how change can be attained. Sustainability is a prime example. In countries as diverse as China, the UAE, the UK, and the US, new government-sponsored developments are the benchmarks for the value of an integrated approach to sustainable design. Yet government is also intensely aware of the private sector's efforts to ensure that buildings and their settings contribute fully to human and organizational performance. As life grows more mobile, the government workforce is changing. This creates unprecedented opportunities to use office real estate especially in new and better ways.

This is the next frontier, not just in terms of securing a higher return on public investment, but also in meeting the aggressive carbon-reduction targets that government has admirably set for itself. Unlike private sector organizations, even ones operating at a global scale, government has the ability to test the actual results of its initiatives and policies. As a long-term owner and user of the built environment, it has every incentive to invest up front in order to reap benefits downstream. By documenting these benefits, government encourages the private sector to follow its lead. And only government can create the incentives that enable society to abandon short-term habits that no longer serve. Only government can create, maintain, and modernize the crucial infrastructure on which society depends. Airports; local and intercity transit; high-speed rail; policies that encourage compact, walkable growth and discourage sprawl: this is government at work. Gensler is proud to be its partner, everywhere in the world.

M. Arthur Gensler Jr., FAIA, FIIDA, RIBA
Founder and Chairman, Gensler

Andrew P. Cohen, FAIA
David Gensler
Diane Hoskins, FAIA
Executive Directors, Gensler

Introduction by Vernon Mays

Government increasingly touches our lives. As the role of the public sector expands, there is a growing need for modern, high-performance buildings to house government employees and provide them with the increasingly sophisticated technology-supported workspace they require to do their jobs. In the same way that public companies are accountable to their shareholders, government is accountable to the citizens it serves. Its use of public funds makes it especially aware of the need to evaluate and justify its choices. As a result, government is often in the forefront in using empirical evidence to inform design decisions. A standout in this respect is America's General Services Administration (GSA), which collects and interprets data on a variety of performance criteria, including energy use, carbon emissions, water consumption, main-tenance costs, and employee satisfaction. As a result, new and renovated federal office buildings are setting national benchmarks.

While GSA has aggressively implemented green design since the 1970s, legislation passed in 2007 set ambitious new energy-reduction targets for government buildings. In 2009, GSA established the Office of Federal High-Performance Green Buildings; GSA has made it clear that *high performance* includes not only the buildings, but also their impact on the organizations they house and the people they support. The priority that governments place on high-performing buildings is focusing renewed attention on energy efficiency and the use of "smart" technologies—both of which are being implemented to meet legislated greenhouse gas–emission targets and reduce long-term operating costs. Energy efficiency goes beyond just installing modern HVAC systems. It takes in technologies such as high-performance glass, which allows government buildings to convey a sense of welcoming and openness to its constituents. Measures like high-efficiency lighting, under-floor air-distribution systems, and ground source heat pumps reduce agencies' costs while setting a positive example for their communities.

Supporting mobility in the workplace

Sustainable work settings are on the increase because workers favor them. While healthy environments are important, there is also a strong design component to workplace effectiveness. Access to daylight, for example, often goes hand in hand today with an open-plan workspace that fosters collaboration. Through research, Gensler has shown the correlation between high-performance workplace design and organizational success metrics such as productivity, employee engagement, innovation, and financial performance.

The firm's survey-based Workplace Performance Index (WPI) is a leading measurement and analysis tool that helps organizations to quantify workplace effectiveness and then improve it.

Feedback received through the WPI informs Gensler's understanding of how the workplace supports productive activity and, in turn, which physical changes in the workplace are having an influence on worker productivity. Research conducted by Gensler and others confirms the link between workplace design quality and a wide range of outcomes, including the health of employees, the ability of the organization to attract and retain people, absenteeism, how well teams achieve results, speed of communication, and the image an organization projects to its customers.

In particular, recognition of the need to support collaboration is leading to more open work environments and the inclusion of a wider variety of spaces that foster teamwork and informal conversation, networking, and knowledge-sharing. Individual, focused work and large scheduled meetings are less important to many organizations, government agencies included, as more workers embrace mobility. This emphasis on end-user performance is already yielding tangible results. For example, post-occupancy evaluation of federal government buildings designed by Gensler reveals that, compared to the facilities they replaced, the new work settings showed improved levels of collaboration, individual work effectiveness, and workplace satisfaction.

OPPOSITE •• The Department of Homeland Security's new sustainable office building performed so well in a 2008 post-occupancy evaluation that GSA cited it as a benchmark for federal buildings.

Worker mobility is changing how the private sector thinks about real estate. The public sector isn't far behind. Many agencies of the federal government (particularly the US) have actively promoted telework—as have states such as Arizona, California, Texas, Georgia, and Virginia—in order to increase worker productivity, lower carbon emissions, and reduce worker stress associated with commuting. A GSA-funded study of mobility that Gensler carried out with workplace researchers Paul Heath and Judith Heerwagen showed that although the federal government defines *telework* as "working from home," many federal agencies now apply the term to mobile work of all kinds. Mobility is here, and the federal government's carbon-footprint mandates are likely to increase its importance. GSA has the highest bar in this respect, and some observers believe it cannot realistically meet it with sustainable building practices alone—that GSA will have to embrace mobility's potential for real-estate leverage, as the private sector is doing, to hit the aggressive carbon-reduction targets set for it.

Gensler has consistently found a 30- to 40-percent space-utilization rate across the US office workplace. The assumption that every employee should have an assigned desk is also challenged by changing work modes, which put more emphasis on small-group interaction. In recent years, companies like Hewlett-Packard have cut their office workspace in half by exploiting the leverage that mobility offers to increase density of use across the workplace. GSA is only gradually increasing its space utilization and consolidating its real estate. A few federal agencies with well-established telework programs have reduced their office footprint by implementing shared workspaces, electronic document access to limit the need for paper filing space, and wireless connectivity that enables mobile workers to choose from a variety of available spaces when they are in the office. The US Office of Personnel Management is establishing an advisory group of federal agencies to review federal policies on telework and mobility. Gensler is assisting in this effort by identifying global best practices. The goal is to help federal agencies overcome barriers to mobility and find better ways to accommodate mobile workers.

The federal government's security concerns have been largely overcome as an obstacle to mobile work, but security persists as an important issue for public agencies in the post-9/11 era. In addition to securing confidential or classified data, federal agencies have a heightened need for work settings that protect people and property. Gensler is a leader in this arena, having worked with the Office of the Chief Architect to develop GSA's *Site Security Design Guide*, a handbook for the private sector that explains how to design buildings to meet GSA's high security standards for federal agency tenants.

Strategic real-estate management
Gensler's expertise in strategic real-estate and portfolio planning has been an effective resource for supporting organizational culture, goals, and mission for governments at all scales. The firm has helped the US government tackle massive real-estate projects including the strategic planning required of the US Department of Defense to comply with Base Realignment and Closure recommendations. The scale

and complexity of this effort, involving more than 11 million square feet of real estate in 101 buildings, required Gensler's ability to manage a wide range of data and organize key stakeholders. To generate forecasts and provide decision-making tools, the firm developed a customized database to track, manage, and simulate real-estate scenarios and their potential financial impacts.

Local governments also struggle with real-estate issues, particularly as their staffs outgrow aging buildings that are often undersized and inadequately equipped for 21st-century urban management. Gensler recently completed a facilities needs assessment for the city of San Diego, whose workforce is five times the capacity of its aging City Administration Building. Analysis of the city's workforce and real-estate needs led to recommendations that identified which workers need to be located downtown and how a new facility could improve the way the city does business.

The importance of design excellence
Through the early 20th century, there was a widely shared consensus that government buildings would strive for gravitas and draw on tradition to emphasize continuity and timelessness. Especially in the US in the decades after World War II, an emphasis on frugality with taxpayer money led to "functional" public buildings that later proved to be inflexible and at odds with their communities' desire for a greater sense of place and civic presence. (Many universities and colleges went through a similar period.) To its lasting credit, GSA's Public Buildings Service has led the way in reversing this trend. GSA's Design

Excellence program invited architects to use the federal government's significant new building and renovation projects as occasions for design of the highest quality. Gensler is working on its second Design Excellence project, the renovation of a federal courthouse in Honolulu. The first, the Richard B. Russell Federal Building renovation in Atlanta, is this book's opening case study.

Government has every reason to take a longer view. Much that government does is necessarily urgent, but the majority of its buildings are intended for decades of use, housing activities that will surely change over time. Efficiency, flexibility, durability, and ease of updating and reuse are crucial. Design excellence has to be measured in light of endurance, not just when the ribbon is cut on opening day. This is real sustainability.

At Gensler, design excellence is understood to be more than skin deep. It impacts end-user perceptions of comfort, performance, and job satisfaction. It expresses the image and identity of public agencies as their communities perceive them, at a time when government is increasingly called on to embody public values and aspirations. More to the point, it shows how they can be realized here and now.

Vernon Mays is a writer, based in Richmond, Virginia. He is editor at large of *Architect*, and the former editor of *Inform*, the magazine of the Virginia Society of the American Institute of Architects.

FLOYD C. EILER
POLICEMAN ~ 12/12/86

JAMES P. WYLIE
PATROLMAN ~ 5/27/69

FRANK E. CORLEY
POLICEMAN ~ 08/24/1924

WILLIAM H. MARPLE
POLICEMAN ~ 02/17/1929

CHARLES E. JOHNSON
LIEUTENANT ~ 5/74/1971

WILLIAM G. BROWN
POLICEMAN ~ 05/01/1958

E. J. BICKEL
POLICEMAN ~ 05/20/1971

RAY N. HUNT
PATROLMAN ~ 08/05/1955

JAMES C. BEYER
POLICE OFFICER ~ 05/07/1988

JACK W. HARRIS
POLICEMAN ~ 02/01/1916

CHRISTY L. HAMILTON
POLICE OFFICER ~ 02/22/1994

DAVID L. HOFMEYER
POLICE OFFICER ~ 12/17/1988

BOBBY LEACK
POLICE OFFICER ~ 08/05/1983

GARY W. MURAKAMI
POLICEMAN ~ 03/28/1968

JOSE L. CASTELLANOS
POLICEMAN ~ 03/05/1959

DAVID C. SCHMID

National projects

Designing government's new benchmarks

Governments now use their public building programs to set new standards for excellence. Gensler's design response addresses their need for higher performance and their desire for civic presence.

Gensler's commissions to design major government headquarters reflect its understanding that they are not only significant real-estate investments, but also opportunities to make the organizations that will occupy them much more effective. This was true for GCHQ, the Government Communications Headquarters, in the UK. Gensler's new campus for GCHQ brings together a staff that was scattered among 50 different buildings. Secure, sustainable, and sophisticated in its open planning and technology support, GCHQ is a model for government campuses in Europe.

Gensler's experience with national government also includes two far-reaching initiatives of the US General Services Administration (GSA). The first of these, conceived with Robert Peck of GSA's Public Buildings Service—initially as a way to expedite improvements to building security in the post-9/11 era—became known as the First Impressions program. The goal was to transform federal buildings to raise their quality and make them safe, welcoming. This national program, which Gensler helped lead, addressed circulation issues, upgraded security, and improved the image and identity of federal agencies by redesigning their buildings' public entries and plazas.

Gensler's second GSA initiative was the WorkPlace 20•20 program, also sponsored by the Public Buildings Service. Gensler leveraged its exceptional knowledge of office building and workspace design to play a central role in developing this groundbreaking federal workplace reinvention and evaluation effort. The aim is to tailor the design of federal office buildings and their work settings to the agency's mission, goals, and organizational strategies. The first wave of WorkPlace 20•20 projects, including several designed by Gensler, is now up and running. A GSA-sponsored research team has verified their higher individual and organizational performance compared to the facilities they replaced.

In many ways, WorkPlace 20•20 reflects strategic planning and design practices already employed by Gensler in its work with commercial clients. It establishes a strategic mission focus for the workplace, helping people think about how and why they work—not just where. It also challenges federal agencies to launch a workplace redesign by embracing the underlying mission and goals of their organizations. This process opens the door to create value by linking building investments with business and behavior. It also provides innovative change management strategies so space can become a catalyst for change.

GSA took an early lead in requiring federal building projects to achieve LEED Silver certification or better, a trajectory that led Congress in 2009 to authorize GSA to spend $4.5 billion developing or renovating federal buildings for higher performance. A 2008 Pacific Northwest National Laboratory study found that the best-performing buildings in GSA's portfolio take a fully integrated approach to sustainable design—addressing site development, water savings, energy efficiency, materials selection, and indoor environmental quality. One of the best performers, the Department of Homeland Security (DHS) building in Omaha, Nebraska, was designed by Gensler. The DHS building performs well across all categories, with an ENERGY STAR rating in the top one-third of the sample buildings. In addition, it incorporates strategies, such as rainwater harvesting and low-flow fixtures in restrooms, that resulted in water costs 66 percent below the national average.

With oversight of several hundred million square feet of mainly office real estate, GSA—like equivalent government agencies elsewhere in the world—is uniquely positioned to influence other organizations. This includes not only state and local governments, which look to GSA as a benchmark, but also the corporations and institutions that depend on GSA's national database of building performance, with its own portfolio as the source. Its willingness to evaluate buildings and work settings objectively to prove or disprove the value of current methods of workplace planning and integrated sustainable design is also a tremendous service. Gensler has partnered with GSA since 2008 to publicize these findings.

Outside the US, international airports are often the purview of national government. Singapore Changi Airport's Terminal 2, a stunning and ambitious renovation of a decade-old building, speaks to government's recognition of the association people make between a nation's civic architecture and its claims to leadership on the world stage. For a city-state like Singapore, Changi Airport is the gateway—the first and last thing visitors experience. Without ever crossing the line into ostentation, Gensler's redesign of Terminal 2 creates the world-class settings that help make Changi the leading international airport in the region.

A major new government complex like GCHQ and a newly renovated one like the Richard B. Russell Federal Building similarly combine the higher performance that governments require with the presence appropriate to major works of civic architecture. They also resolve the need for security with the apparently opposed desire for openness. No government can afford to present itself as a fortress, or to wall off the public it serves, so much creative effort goes into resolving this dilemma.

Gensler has saved the US government large sums—$30 million in the case of the massive US Patent and Trademark Office campus—by solving issues like consolidation lease-exiting. Constantly exploring new delivery methods, Gensler counts GCHQ, Europe's largest private finance initiative (PFI) development, as one of its prominent successes. To be the architect partner of government today means being a strategist, an innovator, a problem solver, and—most of all—a trusted advisor, willing to put the public interest first.

OPPOSITE •• **The Drug Enforcement Agency's eco-friendly office building is designed to engage the community with such features as a public lobby, a top-floor terrace, and a corner garden of drought-resistant native plants.**

Richard B. Russell Federal Building

Office Building and Courthouse Modernization
Atlanta, Georgia, USA

A project for the US General Services Administration

GSA

In brief

Type: Building modernization
Completed: 2007
Size: 1.25 million sf
Height: 26 stories
Green factor: ENERGY STAR rated

Designed in the 1970s, the Richard B. Russell Federal Building exemplified the public architecture of that era. The plaza fronting the building, a desolate public space interrupted by temporary barriers, was virtually unused by government employees and the community. Faced with new security requirements in the wake of 9/11, the US General Services Administration (GSA) decided to modernize the building under the Design Excellence program. Gensler designed a welcoming entry pavilion that humanizes the plaza and resolves the building's security issues, and brought the building and its courtrooms to current standards of performance and security. The design excellence GSA sought was achieved with modest but strategic interventions that renewed the 30-year-old building and restored its civic presence.

OPPOSITE •• Recalling other landmark urban plazas in the federal portfolio, the new entry pavilion is a strong sculptural form set against the uniform backdrop of the original tower. OVERLEAF •• Contemporary, computer-controlled bending technology enabled fabricators to create the complex curves of the panels that enclose one side of the pavilion.

The Russell Federal Building is a notable example of the efforts being made by GSA's Public Buildings Service to refurbish older federal buildings. GSA asked Gensler to work with the 1970s modernist context of the existing building. For the entry pavilion, the design team treated the main building as a backdrop, juxtaposing a more sculptural element with its straight-forward geometric grid pattern. This recalls some of the federal government's most successful urban plazas, also anchored by a sculpture. The pavilion's white metal panels complement the existing structure while establishing a fresh new vocabulary. The play of light on the flat wall, curved plane, and glass of the pavilion makes for an easily recognized entrance and gives warmth and movement to what had been a cold and lifeless urban space.

Visitors approach along a flanking ramp or directly up a set of monumental steps that evoke the grandeur of government buildings in America's past. Both routes lead to a new public plaza elevated several feet higher than the old plaza to extend the security perimeter. On the plaza, a new domed skylight of blast-proof design replaces an earlier cone-shaped one. The new sky-light's broad, rounded surface is a counterpoint to the pavilion's strong verticality. Green lawn panels incor-porate security between the building and a grove of trees. These moves make the pavilion the centerpiece of a plaza that, with its park-like character, welcomes visitors even as it secures the building's perimeter.

With the relocation of building security to the entry pavilion, the ground-floor lobby was renovated, along with office-floor elevator lobbies, public restrooms, and other public areas, to improve their functionality and the user experience. Working with a courtroom consult-ant, Ricci Greene Associates, Gensler renovated the existing Magistrate and District courtrooms and added three new courtrooms. They now meet current US Courts standards in their appearance and functionality. Upgraded systems and glazing improve the building's energy performance and provide blast resistance.

Green facts

ENERGY STAR rating	20-year savings in energy costs
78	**18**%

Renovation facts

Original building entries	Current building entries
8	**1**
Upgraded courtrooms	**New federal courtrooms**
13	**3**

OPPOSITE •• **Replacing eight different entries, Gensler created a welcoming, secure, single-point visitor screening area and employee entrance.**

Site plan and ground-level floor plan

1: New specimen trees
2: Metal panel wall
3: New security desk with x-ray and metal detectors
4: New glass-enclosed connector
5: Granite steps
6: Skylight
7: Raised granite benches
8: Raised planters
9: Lawn panel
10: Seat wall

OPPOSITE, TOP ●● The metal-clad pavilion occupies an elevated platform to enhance security; panels of green lawn were added to extend the boundaries of the secure perimeter. OPPOSITE, BOTTOM ●● The plaza's paving configuration funnels pedestrian traffic toward the entry pavilion. OVERLEAF ●● Both the new and renovated courtrooms incorporate up-to-date technology.

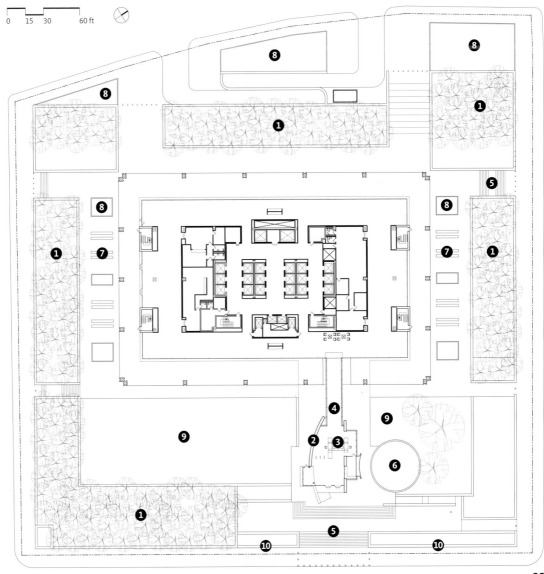

Department of Homeland Security

Office Building and Service Center
Omaha, Nebraska, USA

A project for the US General Services Administration

GSA

In brief

Type: Office building
Completed: 2005
Size: 86,000 sf
Height: 1 story
LEED NC Gold

The goal of the US Department of Homeland Security (DHS) for its Omaha office building was to create a user-friendly, productive, and sustainable workplace that met stringent security requirements. By redeveloping a brownfield site along the Missouri River, DHS also reclaimed part of the city's riverfront for public use. Pacific Northwest National Laboratory's 2008 study of sustainable federal buildings ranked DHS Omaha among the top two for overall performance. In reporting these findings, the US General Services Administration's Public Buildings Service pointed to the building as a benchmark. Housing two different groups involved with immigration and security, DHS Omaha serves visitors and provides secure and supportive office space and indoor and outdoor amenities for federal employees.

OPPOSITE •• **The LEED-Gold office building features a high-performance skin with insulated aluminum frames and low-e glass. The white membrane roof reduces energy costs by reflecting the sun's heat away from the building. OVERLEAF** •• **The high-bay public lobby, rhythmic colonnade, and projecting canopy on the west façade present a recognizable landmark easily seen from the entrance on Abbott Drive.**

The public face of DHS Omaha—an entry vestibule with reception desk and seating, is designed to meet GSA's "First Impressions" credo of providing a warm welcome for visitors. Screening devices at the security checkpoint are an integral part of the design, making it less intrusive and providing a smooth transition to the secure areas of the building. Federal employees have a separate, secure outdoor courtyard, entirely enclosed by the building, shielded from casual access and view. The landscaped space also helps bring daylight into the interior of the building.

A wide array of green design strategies was implemented to make the building perform optimally. Water conservation was a key area of emphasis. Rainwater collected from the roof is stored in two 7,500-gallon tanks inside the building. This system, in combination with native plantings around the building and high-efficiency irrigation, treats 100 percent of storm water runoff before it leaves the site. The building's integrated energy strategy combines a geothermal heat pump with such building features as a high-performance window-wall using insulated aluminum frames and low-emission glass. Super-insulated walls also help maintain consistent indoor temperatures without expending energy.

The effectiveness of these techniques was borne out in a comprehensive post-occupancy evaluation of 12 federal buildings commissioned by the GSA. All 12 buildings, including DHS in Omaha, were designed with sustainability in mind. The measures studied included environmental performance, financial metrics, and occupant satisfaction. The DHS building performed well across all categories. Its ENERGY STAR rating (85) was in the top third of the sample group. And its water costs tallied 66 percent below the baseline established jointly by the Building Owners and Managers Association International and the International Facility Management Association (BOMA/IFMA). Overall, the DHS building was found to be 66 percent more energy efficient than an average office building of comparable size. Of particular note is the building's scoring on occupant satisfaction—how employees rate their workplace in terms of air quality, cleanliness, thermal comfort, acoustics, and lighting. DHS performed highest in this category among all buildings in the study.

RIGHT AND OPPOSITE ●● The building lobby conveys a sense of openness and warmth to visitors, yet is visually separated from staff work areas for security purposes. Wood panels that wrap up and over the reception area are made of bamboo, a renewable material.

Floor plan

1: Main entry
2: First impressions security screening
3: Information and waiting lobby
4: Secured courtyard
5: Secured covered parking
6: Loading/receiving
7: Typical office space
8: Detention rooms
9: Sally port

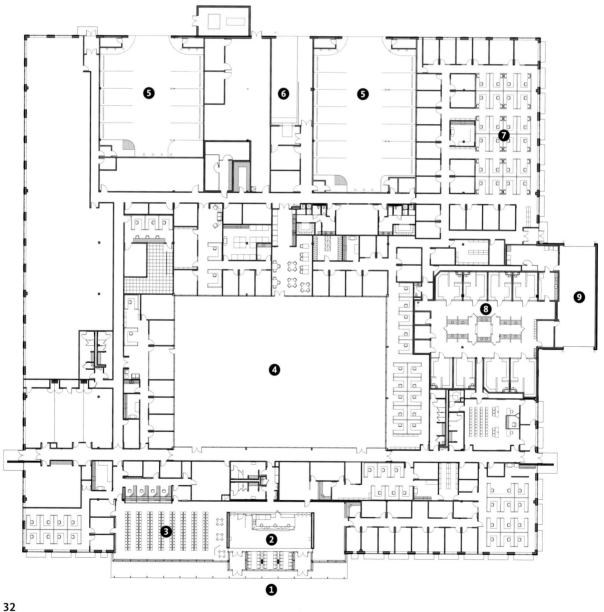

Green facts

ENERGY STAR rating (2008)	Energy use vs. ASHRAE 90.1
85	**66**%

Building's use of "green" power	Aggregate water-use savings
50%	**77**%

Performance facts

Operating costs vs. industry baseline	User satisfaction with thermal comfort
42%	**90**%

User satisfaction with acoustics	User satisfaction with building
90%	**95**%

U.S. GREEN BUILDING COUNCIL
LEED GOLD
USGBC™

Design fact

Use of FSC-certified wood products

50%

BELOW •• The central courtyard brings daylight to the interior office space and gives employees a secure outdoor area for breaks. The use of native plants reduces the need for irrigation.

OVERLEAF •• Light shelves spanning the front of the building's glass façade bounce daylight deep into the building, while rooftop skylights pour natural light into the deep recesses of the building.

Government Communications Headquarters

High Security Office Campus
Cheltenham, Gloucestershire, UK

In brief

Type: Headquarters campus
Completed: 2004
Size: 1.1 million sf
Height: 3 stories
BREEAM Very Good

Work is top secret at the UK's Government Communications Headquarters (GCHQ), an agency similar to America's National Security Agency. Some 55 years after the end of World War II, GCHQ occupied 50 buildings, many dating back to the 1950s. By consolidating into a new campus, GCHQ anticipated that they could improve their organizational effectiveness and reduce operating costs. Turning to the private sector, GCHQ held a design-led competition among qualified consortiums to deliver the new campus. Teamed with Carillion, Gensler designed the winning scheme. Located at Benhall in Cheltenham, the GCHQ campus is one of Europe's largest public buildings, and the largest project developed using the private finance initiative (PFI) method. The result is a modern, secure office complex that supports the effective delivery of intelligence.

ABOVE •• At the new campus's dedication, Gensler's Chris Johnson offers an informed view to Her Majesty Queen Elizabeth II. OPPOSITE •• The headquarters, popularly known as "The Doughnut," features a circular floor plan that reduced construction costs through the repetition of design elements and construction techniques. OVERLEAF •• Site efficiency is maximized with parking located close to the buildings and surplus land freed up for residential use.

Site plan

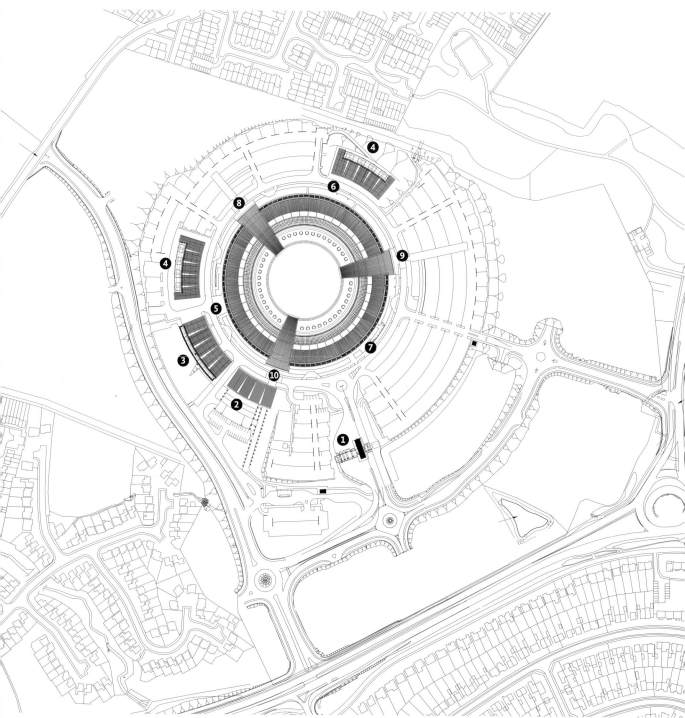

0   100   200   400 ft

1: Gatehouse
2: Visitor center
3: Logistics building
4: Services building
5: Block A

6: Block B
7: Block C
8: Link Block AB
9: Link Block BC
10: Link Block AC

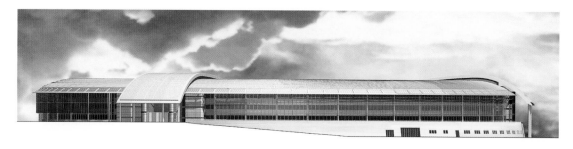

GCHQ sought a new headquarters campus that combined flexible, productive workspace with absolute security, integrating separate operating units and giving them a sense of shared purpose, even as it supported their individual needs. GCHQ has long ties with Cheltenham, and there was a desire by both to fit the campus into the city fabric. Indeed, Cheltenham and its citizens were vocal advocates for the project during the competition, when sites elsewhere were in play. Led by Carillion, the winning consortium included Gensler as building architect and workplace designer. Under PFI, the winner builds and operates the headquarters for 30 years, at which point GCHQ takes it over.

Gensler's winning design for GCHQ organized three identical, three-story office buildings as a secure ring around a landscaped courtyard. This configuration, quickly dubbed "The Doughnut," provides GCHQ employees with a protected space, shielded by the complex itself against external threats. Cotswold stone forms a bastion-like base that anchors the campus in the local setting, while planes of reinforced glass set at different angles prevent outsiders from seeing into the buildings.

The complex encloses a flexible, supportive, high-performance workplace. The open plan workspaces promote a collaborative culture by encouraging informal interaction and knowledge sharing. Even the shape of the building supports this goal: no one is more than a five minutes' walk from any other colleague in the building. The circular plan also allows for easy reconfiguration to accommodate the changing requirements of work teams, which have the ability to expand horizontally and vertically.

Lighting and ventilation are key aspects of GCHQ's sustainable strategies and user experience. A glass-roofed internal street running through the complex connects its different work units. This passageway does more than aid circulation—it is the lungs of GCHQ, bringing daylight to the interior, providing natural ventilation, and creating a variety of settings where staff can enjoy lunch or gather informally in small groups. GCHQ's circular shape reduces the floor-to-wall ratio by 20 percent over similarly sized office buildings, lowering development costs and reducing internal temperature variations. As a result, GCHQ's office energy costs are about 40 percent lower than they were prior to consolidation.

Level-3 floor plan

1: Office
2: Internal street
3: Courtyard
4: Courtyard access
5: Block A
6: Block B
7: Block C
8: Entrance

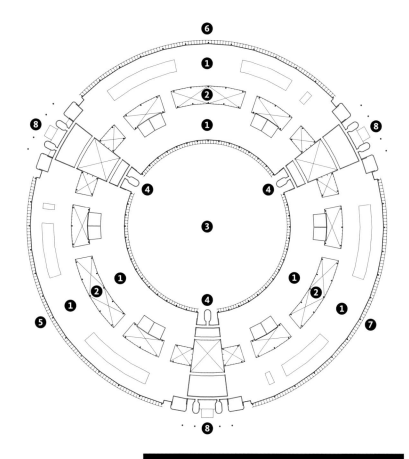

Typical section

1: Office
2: Internal street
3: Courtyard
4: Ring road
5: Computer hall
6: Workshops
7: Plant
8: External roof plant

OPPOSITE •• In addition to aiding internal circulation, the building's glass-roofed internal street fills the building with daylight, promotes natural ventilation, and offers a variety of spaces where staff can eat lunch or meet informally.

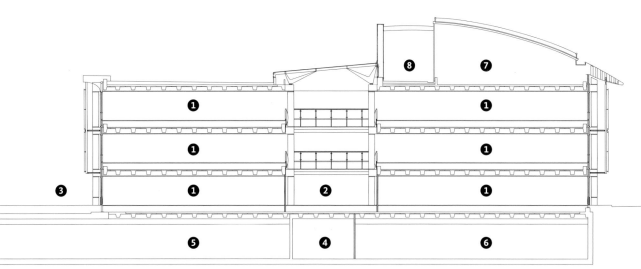

ABOVE •• The high-performance, double-skin exterior wall is one of several energy strategies—in addition to displacement raised floors and chilled beams—that are integral to the building.

BELOW •• A large courtyard, "the hole in the Dough-nut," is a secure retreat with places for outdoor dining. OPPOSITE •• Vertical circulation and access to the courtyard are provided where the separate sections of the headquarters join.

Design fact

Diameter of GCHQ ring

656 ft

Green facts

Recycled wood in desk/table surfaces

90%

Energy savings vs. previous HQ

40%

Singapore Changi Airport

Terminal 2 Renovation
Changi, Singapore, RS

In brief

Type: Passenger terminal
Completed: 2006
Size: 3.8 million sf
Height: 2 stories
Green factor: Sustainably designed

Singapore Changi Airport has long ranked among the top airports in the world, but new competitors in the region are an ongoing threat to its high standing. This led Changi to stage an international competition to renew and upgrade Terminal 2, which had only been in operation for 11 years. Gensler and its Singapore partner, RSP Architects Planners & Engineers, were chosen. The result is a virtually new terminal—with a dramatic new entrance canopy, an upgraded ticketing lobby, and vastly expanded passenger amenities that convey Changi's determination to be the international airport of choice for a new generation of travelers in the region.

OPPOSITE •• To enhance the terminal's shopping and dining opportunities, the transit mall was expanded with 30,000 square feet of new space overlooking the apron. **OVERLEAF ••** Protection from tropical rainstorms was provided for travelers when a dramatic glass canopy was added to the terminal's main entry. Its elegant form recalls large-scale bamboo leaves.

One driver for Terminal 2's upgrade was the need to accommodate the next generation of long-haul aircraft, like the Airbus A380. Increasing the passenger-handling capacity was a key objective—one that afforded the opportunity to bring every aspect of the passenger's experience to a best-in-class standard. The existing terminal suffered from the lack of an effective shelter from tropical rainstorms at the curbside drop-off for departing passengers. Taking inspiration from tropical plants and their beautiful leaves, Gensler designed a cantilevered canopy that protects travelers from the elements while allowing for increased natural light and views. The use of light-steel members with translucent glass panels brightens what was formerly a dark, forbidding, and unprotected entrance.

Arriving passengers enter through the all-glass, transparent front façade into a brightly sky-lit lobby, crossing over interior bridges that span a tropical garden rising from the arrival level one floor below. This tropical theme is recalled as travelers enter the departure hall, where ticketing counters are organized beneath a sweeping illuminated ceiling of glass panels that form a rhythmic pattern of leaf shapes. Additional daylight is brought deep into the terminal via a louvered skylight that runs the length of the terminal at the threshold to the immigration processing area.

The new terminal also enhances and maximizes the commercial opportunities of retail shopping and food and beverage service. Gensler remodeled and expanded the existing retail space, the World Clock Plaza, to create the stylish new Transit Mall. Upscale retailers who once shared shelf space with a variety of mid-price goods in a generic retail setting now are housed in individual boutiques tailored exclusively to their brands. Gensler developed design guidelines for the shop fronts to ensure their cohesiveness, and created new space for restaurants on the airside of the terminal in a new soaring, glass-enclosed "living room" built above the terminal's apron. This 30,000-square-foot addition provides new sources of revenue for the airport while providing a gallery with panoramic views of the runways and planes.

Performance facts

Annual passenger-handling capacity	First-year increase in retail sales
22m	**67**%

Design facts

Length of new entry canopy	Aircraft capacity (terminal jetway)
820ft	**35**

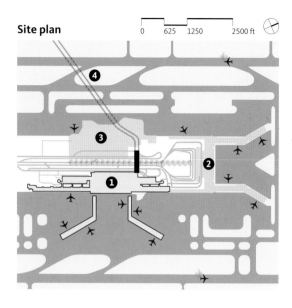

0   625   1250   2500 ft

BELOW •• Terminal 2's modernization encompassed a
new entrance canopy, an upgraded ticketing lobby,
and myriad passenger amenities, features that make
Changi the standout among international airports.
OPPOSITE •• A dark and unprotected entry was
replaced with a soaring steel-and-glass enclosure.
PAGES 56–57 •• Broad walkways at the terminal
entrances bridge large openings that bring daylight
to the arrivals level below.

1: Terminal 2
2: Terminal 1
3: Terminal 3
4: Airport rail connection

Terminal elevation and sections

1: Exterior canopy
2: Glass curtain wall
3: Departures entry vestibules
4: Arrivals exiting vestibules
5: Restaurants
6: Glowing glass ceiling "leaves"
7: Information/currency exchange
8: Ticketing islands (not part of renovation)
9: Information
10: Baggage claim

Landside Arrivals/Departures elevation

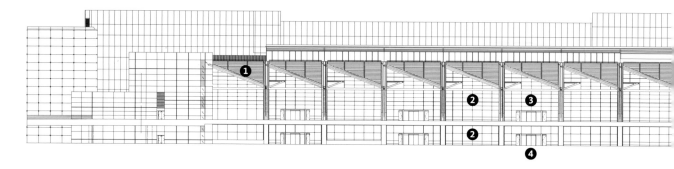

Main Terminal Ticketing Hall section

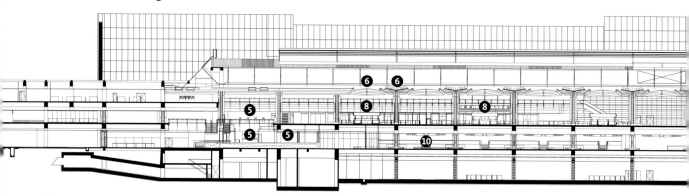

Traverse section of Arrivals/Departures

1: Skylight
2: Louvers
3: Canopy
4: Teak columns
5: Curtain wall
6: Arrivals
7: Departures
8: Planting
9: Bridge to departure hall
10: Entry vestibule
11: Back of house

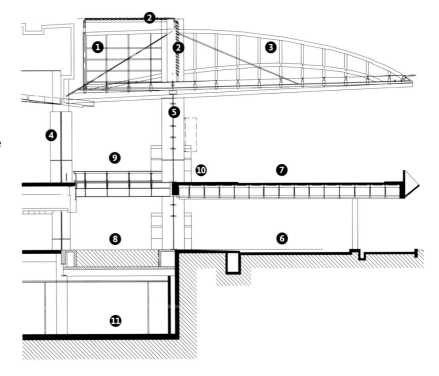

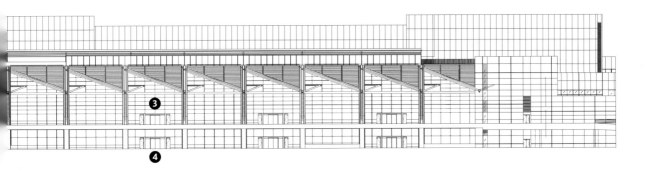

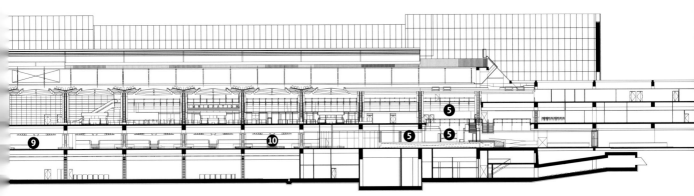

Smithsonian Institution

Collections and Support Center
Landover, Maryland, USA

In brief

Type: Museum exhibitions support center
Completed: 2008
Size: 360,000 sf
Height: 1 story + mezzanine
Green factor: Reuse and daylighting

The public-facing programs of the Smithsonian Institution are supported by an extensive back-of-house operation too large to be housed within the museums. Teaming with owner-developer Trammel Crow, Gensler worked with the Smithsonian to renovate a former furniture showroom and warehouse. With 360,000 square feet of raw space, the building was large enough to consolidate many support functions under one roof. They range from workshops and restoration labs to environmentally controlled collections storage. There is also a security training center and a new mezzanine housing exhibit design and management staff. The design organizes these different functions efficiently, ensuring their security and ease of use. Light, color, and volume are used to create visual interest and a strong sense of community.

ABOVE •• The comprehensive renovation added new on-site workshops for exhibit fabrication and graphic production. OPPOSITE •• A former warehouse was transformed into a lively workplace, with brightly colored walls in the central commons and a convenient counter where breakfast and lunch are set out. OVERLEAF •• Corridors converge on the spacious commons, designed with new skylights and lighting.

The pending expiration of multiple leases prompted the Smithsonian Institution to seek new space where myriad functions could be consolidated under one roof. An empty furniture showroom and warehouse outside of Washington, DC, provided the raw space. Teaming with Trammel Crow, the building's owner-developer, Gensler worked closely with the Smithsonian Institution departments to be housed to design the transformation of the 360,000-square-foot shell into a multifunctional center supporting the Smithsonian's exhibitions program. The functions and facilities added in the renovation include new workshops for fabrication and graphics production, environmentally controlled collections storage, 90,000 linear feet of library shelving, a rare book conservation lab, and a security training center. A new 13,000-square-foot mezzanine houses exhibit design and management staff.

The Center's expansive interior is organized as a series of enclosed blocks placed along the main corridors like buildings along a street. Several corridors converge on a spacious central plaza that serves as the facility's communal gathering space—a place for lunch and large meetings. Skylights cut into the roof bring daylight into the room, supplemented by fluorescent tubes that hang vertically from the ceiling in a playful manner. A steel stair rises from the plaza to the mezzanine, which contains conference rooms, offices, and a room for graphic production. Clustered in the space below it are such services as restrooms, exercise rooms, locker rooms, and showers. The entire facility is served by a six-bay covered loading dock that supports secure, climate-tempered materials handling. The new Center reduced the Smithsonian's operating costs by more than 10 percent while maximizing usable space and enhancing the work environment. The use of a mobile shelving system increased library collections storage capacity by more than 700 percent—from 68,000 to 500,000 volumes.

The project met an aggressive 17-month schedule for design, construction, move-in, and testing for the Smithsonian—a public trust that, while not a federal agency, is chartered by Congress and is 70 percent funded by the US government. Gensler took a collaborative approach to the design-build process, convening regular meetings with Smithsonian users, managers, and facilities staff to ensure effective communication and mutual trust. The build-out cost of the Center averaged $25 per square foot less than the cost of renovating existing leased space—with no disruption to ongoing operations.

Design fact

Amount of linear book shelving

90,000 ft

Performance facts

Operating-cost savings vs. previous facilities	Cost savings vs. upgrading in place
>10%	**25%**

OPPOSITE, TOP •• Stairs in the commons lead to a mezzanine housing graphic production and other workspace. OPPOSITE, BOTTOM •• A blue exhibit wall at the entry also helps first-time visitors locate a suite of training rooms and the library.

First-floor plan

1: Lobby
2: Staff offices
3: Classrooms and training rooms
4: Café
5: Collections workroom
6: Libraries conservation lab
7: Conference rooms
8: Library collections housing
9: Collections storage
10: Wood fabrication shop
11: Metal fabrication shop
12: Model making and staging
13: Large exhibit staging
14: Graphics production bench and staging
15: Shipping and receiving
16: General storage
17: Room for future growth

OPPOSITE •• The use of bright-colored paint, skylights, and lighting humanizes the building and orients people within it.

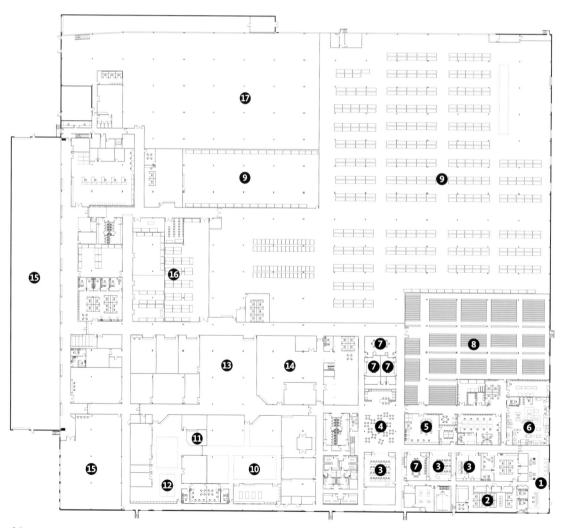

Drug Enforcement Agency

Office Building and Campus
Centennial, Colorado, USA

A project for the US General Services Administration

GSA

In brief

Type: Office building
Completed: 2009
Size: 95,241 sf
Height: 4 stories
LEED NC Silver

This sustainable office building for the Drug Enforcement Agency (DEA), designed by Gensler as part of a developer-led team, addresses what has become a recurring dilemma for government agencies: how to strike the right balance between public access and staff security. To resolve it successfully, Gensler organized the site into public and secure zones. An attractive landscaped buffer between the building and the site perimeter avoids projecting a fortress-like image. The offices inside the facility are sequestered by a welcoming atrium lobby, which is offset from the building's core, allowing security to have a clear and controlling view of the entry. Rather than visually dominating it, security is an integral part of the space—a design strategy Gensler has also applied to airport terminals.

OPPOSITE •• **The building's form was developed by shifting the entrance from the central core to the north end, allowing the lobby to become an expressive, three-story element. ABOVE** •• **The building's native landscape creates a security buffer between the building and the site perimeter and supports sustainability goals by reducing rainwater runoff.**

Strict security regulations required a 100-foot minimum spacing from the perimeter fence to the new DEA office building. Gensler's planning of the 10-acre campus complies with this while shifting most of the security perimeter and open space for future expansion away from public view. The DEA campus is elevated slightly above the intersection of two streets. Near this corner, at the low point of the site, Gensler designed a rain-water holding area as a public garden with native grasses and colorful wildflowers—a visual amenity enjoyed by visitors and employees alike.

The office building's public image is defined by its three-story, glass-enclosed atrium lobby. Strategic placement of the atrium on the end of the building, rather than in the core, gives security officers an opportunity to screen visitors before they enter the occupied shell of the building. In keeping with design guidelines of the US General Services Administration's First Impressions program, the security checkpoint is integrated seamlessly into a reception desk. Employees enter from the east end of the lobby; visitors access it separately from the west. Atop the atrium on the fourth floor, a balcony terrace opens to views to the north and west. Part of the balcony is protected by a canopy; the remainder is shaded partially by the signature steel trellis that angles downward and frames the employee entrance.

Much of the building's west façade is wrapped with glass. The remaining surfaces are composed of a series of solids, voids, and glass shapes that articulate the building's simple form. The rectangular floor plate ensures maximum planning efficiency and interior core elements were kept to a minimum, creating flexibility for expansion and reconfiguration. On each floor, the column-free planning depth of 42 feet maximizes daylight penetration into the offices. Sustainability was achieved inside and out. The parking ratios were reduced significantly to preserve open space and limit the amount of impermeable paving surface. Steel structural members, aluminum window framing, and steel stud-wall framing all contain recycled content. High-performance, low-e glazing reduces solar heat load and glare in the building, while a reflective roof lowers heat gain and reduces the heat island effect of the building.

OPPOSITE •• **Key elements of the entry include 1) a rooftop canopy that creates a sheltered terrace on the fourth floor; 2) the secure lobby with separate entries for visitors and staff; 3) a steel trellis that angles downward to highlight the staff entry; and 4) a high-performance curtain wall framed with aluminum of high-recycled content.**

Green facts

Energy savings vs. conventional	Water-use savings vs. conventional
23%	**50**%
Construction waste kept from landfill	Recycled project materials content
82%	**12**%

Elevations

a: East
b: North
c: West
d: South

OPPOSITE •• Rising above a busy intersection, the building strikes a comfortable balance between public access and staff security. **OVERLEAF** •• Workspaces on each floor have direct visual access to the lobby atrium, which features a north orientation that allows full-height glazing to provide light without glare.

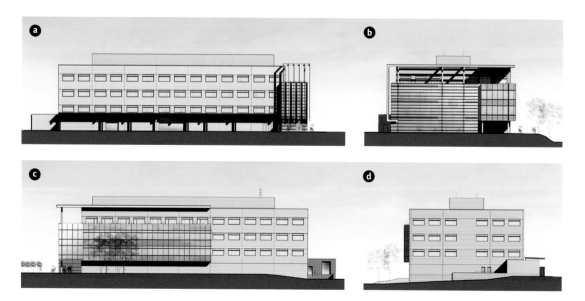

Level-4 floor plan

1: Shared balcony
2: Offset core
3: Executive suite
4: Private offices
5: Private balcony

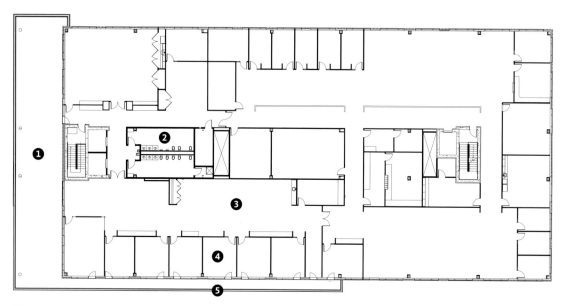

Manchester Magistrates' Courts

Courthouse and Office Building
Manchester, Lancashire, UK

In brief

Type: Courts and office building
Completed: 2004
Size: 155,000 sf
Height: 6 stories
Green factor: Daylighting

Placed at the heart of the city's administrative center, the Manchester Magistrates' Courts is part of a strategy to rejuvenate the area. The midrise complex replaces an obsolete courthouse west of the John Rylands Library, a Victorian landmark. A breakthrough design in terms of efficiency, security, flexibility, and sustainability, the new courthouse is also a welcoming and distinctive civic presence. Its performance benefits from the decision to separate court functions and support offices vertically rather than horizontally. This innovation makes the magistrates' use of the building much more efficient. It also makes for a compact, accessible building that fits well with its context—crucial in an infill project. The central atrium with its bridges connects courts and offices, and brings in daylight.

OPPOSITE •• The courts' main entrance evokes Manchester's celebrated glass-roofed Victorian arcades. It also aligns with the "Processional Way," which links the Alfred Waterhouse–designed Town Hall (1877) with the city's legal district.

The program for Manchester's new Magistrates' Courts called for a building that would challenge conventional procedures and become an integral part of the city's fabric. As realized, the courthouse embraces this concept: It is literally bisected by "The Processional Way," a public promenade that has been a constant element in city master plans since 1945. The design separates the civic court block from the supporting office wing to provide clarity for users. Retail spaces built on the ground floor of the Magistrates' Court support the broad intentions of Spinningfields, a nearby large commercial office development that is stimulating new real-estate investment in the surrounding area.

A glazed atrium slices through the building, providing a protected interior "public street" that delivers visitors, via escalators, to a level-two landing bridge. Magistrates' bridges cross at angles above the internal street, linking their secure offices with the courtrooms (including 18 Magistrates' courts and one Coroner's court). The frequent passage of Magistrates across these bridges animates the interior public space. This division of court and office functions is an innovation in courthouse design, yielding new efficiencies in the hearing of court cases and reducing the distance the magistrates must cover. Waiting areas with city views also lessen tensions for those awaiting trials.

OPPOSITE •• **The atrium separates staff offices from courtrooms, creating an interior public street that connects by escalators to the heart of the building on the second level. BELOW** •• **Seen from outside, the atrium is an inviting, light-filled space. From inside, views look back to the magnificent 1877 Manchester Town Hall in Albert Square.**

By clearly expressing the building's separate functions, Gensler improved the efficiency of the structural and mechanical systems. Two discrete heating and cooling strategies are employed. First, for the court facilities, a displacement ventilation system was installed, with localized heating and ventilation controls operated by the court clerks. Office spaces, on the other hand, demanded a consistently healthy and comfortable environment controlled by individual staff. The narrow floor plate allows for natural ventilation of offices, complemented by mechanical ventilation for spaces deeper within the building interior. External brise soleil on the south façade and louvers on the east and west elevations complete the environmental strategy.

Design facts

Number of courtrooms	Number of holding cells
19	**60**

OPPOSITE •• **Magistrates' bridges crossing at angles within the atrium link courts and offices, and animate the space with activity between court sessions.**

Typical section

1: **Committee room**
2: **Staff dining**
3: **Post-court offices**
4: **Retail**
5: **Atrium bridges**
6: **Escalators**
7: **Family court**
8: **Youth custody court**
9: **Lobby**
10: **Court hall**

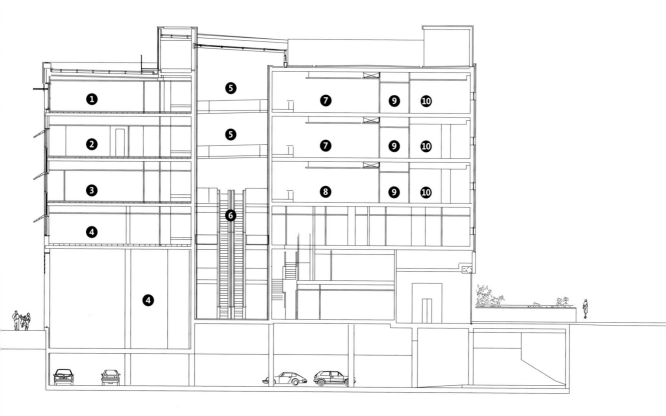

OPPOSITE •• Courtroom waiting areas appear as glass boxes outside, expressing transparency and openness. ABOVE •• The new building has a total of 19 courtrooms.

BELOW, LEFT AND RIGHT •• Head-on and side views of the final design model, showing how the building is organized around the atrium and how it brings light in from the sides.

Botswana Innovation Hub

Research and Development Campus
Gaborone, Botswana

In 2009, the government of Botswana sponsored a design competition for a new Innovation Hub—a world-class R&D campus—in its capital city. Gensler's proposal merges sustainable strategies with design principles tailored to one of Africa's fastest-growing economies. Designed for phased expansion, the new campus draws inspiration from both Botswana's Okavango Delta, an area of abundance in a semi-arid region, and its people, whose creativity and spirit of cooperation have propelled the country's growth. The design anticipates the use of local labor and materials, and incorporates passive cooling, sun shading, and daylighting in a comprehensive, energy-conscious approach. By distributing spaces that support interaction across the campus, the design fosters collaboration among the researchers.

OPPOSITE •• With a fast-growing economy, Botswana is investing in technological advancement, which the Innovation Hub is designed to support, providing flexible R&D and incubator space. **OVERLEAF ••** The complex includes outdoor social and community spaces to foster collaboration among researchers.

The Botswana Innovation Hub draws on the best contemporary thinking on work process, knowledge capture, building technology, materials, building services, and infrastructure to create a rich, supportive habitat for research and development. The campus is planned and designed to deliver a high level of technical support while being firmly rooted in its locale. The competition program called for flexible office and research space complemented by an administration building with offices, a conference facility, meeting rooms, labs, a restaurant, a gymnasium, and support facilities. As part of the plan for phased construction, the initial two buildings gently converge to form a channel that receives residents and visitors while directing people and water on a course that splits into smaller channels and spaces.

The design minimizes cost and complexity while producing the most sustainable result. Roofs, for example, are planted with native scrub, to retain site water and reduce heat gain and glare. They also incorporate solar arrays that produce electricity as they provide shade. The research buildings use five-foot-thick north-facing walls—partially solid for thermal mass and partially hollow for passive ventilation—and semi-transparent south-facing walls to mitigate heat gain and bring glare-free daylight to the interior. They enclose laboratory and office space with a clear span of 59 feet—to promote flexibility in space planning and function. The buildings have generous floor-to-floor heights, providing room for a mezzanine level. Left undivided, they can support light manufacturing, for both prototyping and new business incubation.

The outdoors communicates with the indoors at specific points where the building mass rises off the ground, opening up the ground level and allowing the canteen, café, and entrance to spill out and engage the outdoors. This overflow is enhanced by nearby cooling ponds and other water features, creating a variety of outdoor settings across the campus to support a range of activities and uses. The proposal, which was developed by Gensler architects on a voluntary basis, is a valuable benchmark for other government or NGO-sponsored R&D centers and campuses in developing countries.

OPPOSITE •• **Freestanding canopies provide shade while supporting power-generating photovoltaic arrays. The canopies also help to direct people and segregate public and private activities.**

BELOW •• **Images of the Okavango Delta and its rich ecosystem served as visual metaphors for the design of the Innovation Hub, and ultimately as the specific inspiration for the building forms.**

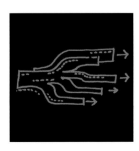

1: Main vehicle entry
2: Main drop-off
3: BIH headquarters
4: Flexible tenant facilities
5: Public entry court
6: Bus stop
7: Community marketplace
8. Discovery trail
9: Outdoor recreation
10: Parking expansion
11: Main entrance
12: Indigenous landscape
13: Parking
14: Photovoltaic roof
15: Green roof
16: Site water–retention ponds

BELOW •• The relationship of the Okavango River, the Kalahari Desert, and the Okavango Delta at the convergence of the two is a key conceptual principle behind the site organization, which channels the flow of people and water.

Concept sketches show a) the transition from desert to delta; b) the buildings' response to the site's radial geometry; c) movement from public to private realms, aided by the buildings; and d) extending the pattern as the Hub grows.

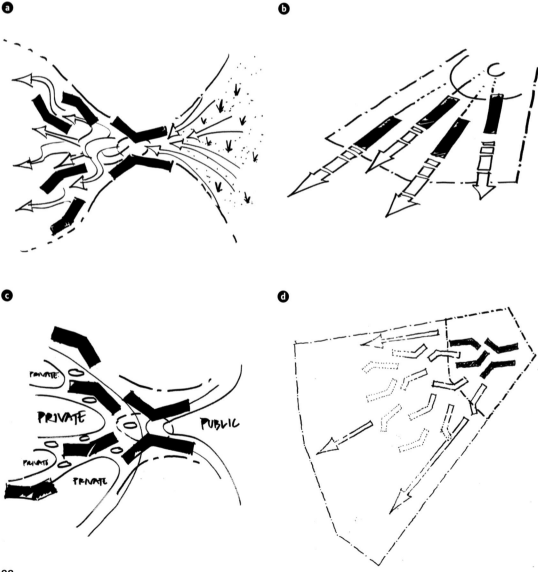

East elevation

South elevation

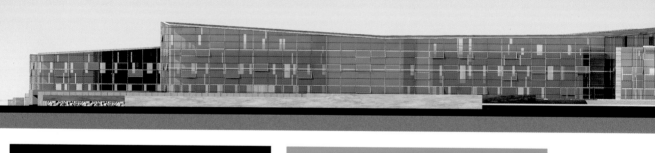

ABOVE AND OPPOSITE •• The design of the building façades reflects the climate and the prevalence of the hot northern sun. The east elevation (above, top) shows the view into the entry courtyard, with a large freestanding canopy. A south-facing curtain wall with integral shading spandrels and low-e glazing is combined with solid north-facing walls using a low-cost rammed earth system of local soil and cement.

Green facts

Solar thermal system share of cooling load

50%

Photovoltaic share of energy demand

20%

Design facts

Lab/office clear-span space

59 ft

Shading spandrels in façade (max.)

50%

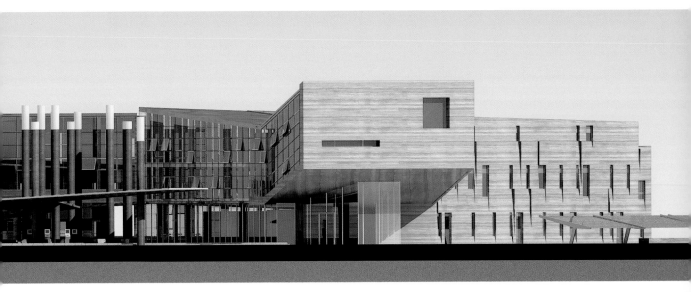

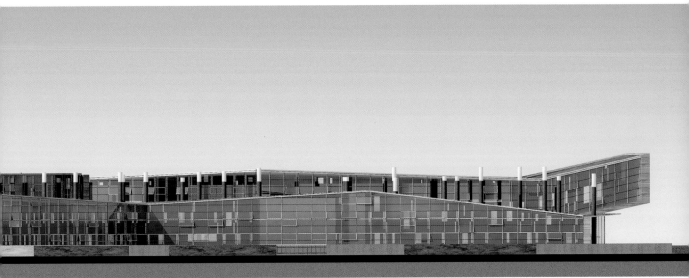

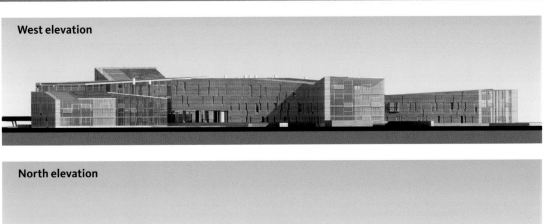

West elevation

North elevation

BELOW ••

Passive strategies help cool the building interiors and reduce energy use. A green roof insulates and lowers heat gain. Northern sunlight is blocked by semi-solid walls, but also converted into electricity by rooftop photovoltaic panels.

a: Solar-thermal radiant floor cooling
b: Natural ventilation with dust traps
c: Vertical fins where required to mitigate low-angle morning and afternoon sun
d: Native scrub–planted green roof retains and filters summer rainfall while insulating building
e: Photovoltaic array supplements up to 20% of building energy requirement
f: Solar-thermal collectors provide hot water for chilled water production for radiant cooling
g: Trombe wall exhausts warmed air to exterior while driving free cooling and cross-ventilation
h: Rock-store chimneys provide cooling of warm morning air

OPPOSITE ••

The materials palette is deliberately restrained. It includes locally produced materials to minimize complexity and cost, maximize sustainability, and maintain the focus on the building form and its interaction with the landscape.

1: Photovoltaic array supplements up to 20% of building energy requirement
2: Native scrub–planted green roof
3: Operable windows
4: Low-e glazing system on south façades
5: Glulam roof beams
6: Structural steel framing system
7: Concrete on metal deck mezzanine
8: Concrete slab on deck below planted roof
9: Site-native soil-colored poured-in-place concrete
10: Glulam wood façade support system
11: Concrete floor slab on grade

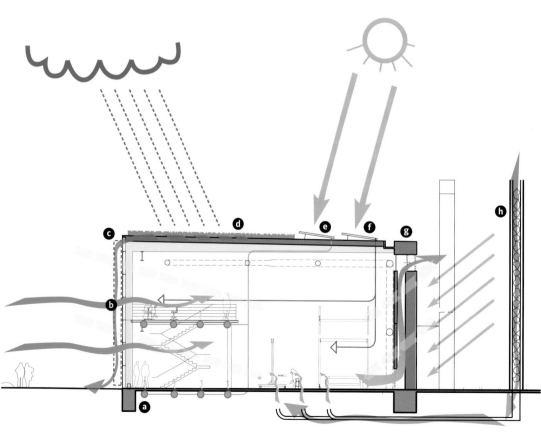

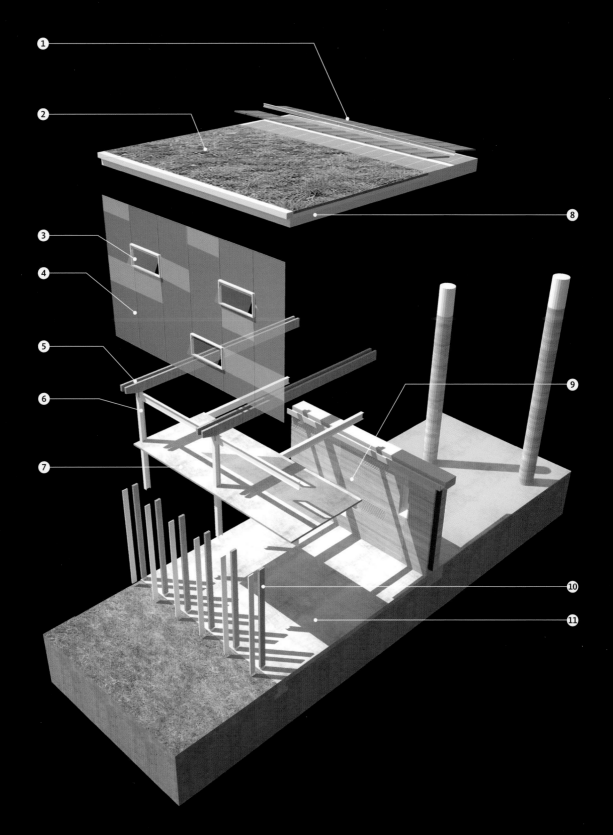

1

2

3

4

5

6

7

8

9

10

11

Patent and Trademark Office

Headquarters Office Campus
Alexandria, Virginia, USA

In brief

Type: Office workplace
Completed: 2005
Height: 10 stories
Size: 2.5 million sf
Green factor: Paperless office

The result of the largest-ever federal government build-ing lease, the US Patent and Trademark Office (USPTO) Headquarters is a 20-acre, eight-building office campus. Gensler carried out the strategic planning and design of the entire 2.5-million-square-foot office workplace to support a staff of 8,000. Gensler's innovative real-estate simulation saved USPTO $30 million in lease-exit costs. Designed with the campus's owner-developer and its core-and-shell architect, the high-performance office campus has the amenities of a small city: a patent search library, a museum, a credit union, a 300-seat cafeteria, two retail cafés, a fitness center, a child care center, a data center, an auditorium and training center, and a health facility.

OPPOSITE •• **The 90,000-square-foot patent search library allows public access to data and records that can help determine eligibility for a new patent. Above it is a state-of-the-art computer search facility.**

OPPOSITE •• Gensler designed wayfinding banners and graphics in the concourse-level walkways that help orient visitors and staff in the eight-building campus.

BELOW ••

1: Amenities to support the staff of 8,000 include the USPTO Federal Credit Union.
2: The full-service cafeteria, seating 300, is a key collaboration and socializing area for staff.
3: Gensler developed a cost-effective wayfinding system using graphics and consistent colors.
4: The fitness center combines energizing, welcoming graphics and durable floors and finishes.

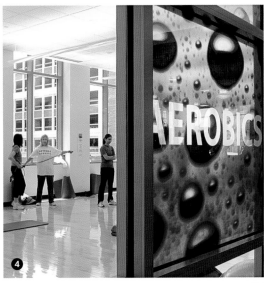

Gensler worked closely with USPTO to understand its unique business process and design a flexible new workplace that shaped the core and shell of each building and influenced the overall layout of the eight-building campus. USPTO's shift from a highly paper-based business process to a more digital system was an important design driver. Flexibility was needed to accommodate new technology and support USPTO's tenancy over the 20-year lease term. To achieve this, Gensler developed a universal plan, applied to all 66 office floors, that lets USPTO rapidly redeploy teams as programs change.

The agency's training center initiates more than 900 new patent examiners yearly through a rigorous training program. Each building includes multi-room conference centers with extensive AV capabilities. Consistent with recent findings on contemporary modes of work, they provide essential collaboration spaces—and a welcoming environment outside the secure upper floors of the complex for meetings with members of the public. These flexible spaces are quickly adapted to user needs. Across the new workplace, the use of durable, cost-effective materials met the requirement for a crisp, modern look, achieved with economy of means. The business-like aesthetic is matched by raised floors, simplifying future technology upgrades. Signage and color simplify wayfinding across the campus.

Prior to design, Gensler developed a facilities management model, termed "The Game," to assist USPTO in relocating and consolidating thousands of employees scattered in 18 facilities with 36 different leases. This management tool analyzed lease expirations, departmental locations, and personnel information to create a plan for short-term lease renewals, long-term relocation phasing, and facilities management in the new facility. Playing "The Game" saved USPTO $30 million. After seven rounds, participating business unit leaders hammered out a relocation strategy that struck an optimal trade-off between reducing lease-exiting costs and minimizing disruption to employees and operations.

Performance facts

Projected cost savings, new campus vs. existing

$98m

Savings from Gensler's lease-exiting strategy

$30m

Reduction in universal enclosed office size

20%

Staff that telework due to hoteling strategy

85%

Green facts

The workplace supports a paperless office strategy, and also supports telework, helping USPTO grow without having to add more space.

Design facts

Ratio of enclosed to open offices

9:1

Total number of office floors

66

Gensler's real-estate simulation used a game-playing approach to help USPTO plan and budget its phased move from Crystal City to the new 8-building headquarters campus in Alexandria, simplifying a complicated lease-exiting plan involving 18 buildings, 36 leases, and 108 floors of office space.

1: Randolph Building
2: Remsen Building
3: Knox Building
4: Jefferson Building
5: Madison West
6: Madison East
7: Elizabeth Townhouse
8: Carlyle Townhouse

● Phase 1
○ Phase 2
● Phase 3
● Phase 4*
● Phase 5

* Phase 4 consolidation occurred at a different site.

Campus plan

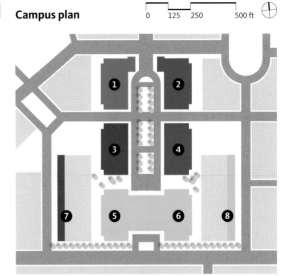

0   125   250   500 ft

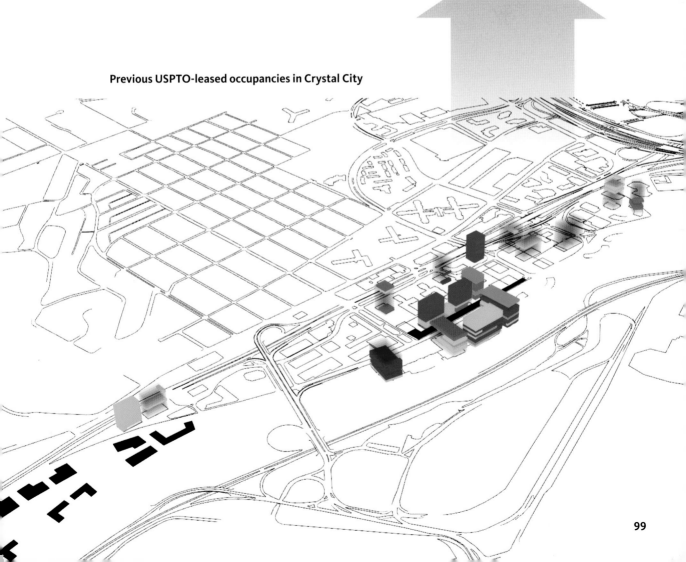

Previous USPTO-leased occupancies in Crystal City

BELOW •• Simple and economical materials met USPTO's clearly defined budget while presenting a contemporary, forward-looking image. In all selections, Gensler emphasized durability and cost-effectiveness. Throughout the large campus, graphic wayfinding devices help people find 1) restrooms, 2) internal offices, 3) departmental floors, and 4) training facilities.

OPPOSITE •• Signatures of notable inventors line the atrium of the public patent search library.

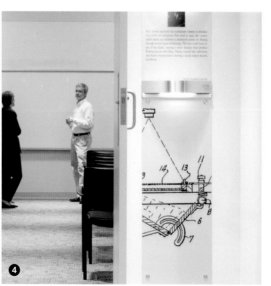

Community projects

Repositioning state and local government

Decades of growth have almost tripled public sector employment in the US at the state and local levels. As budgetary constraints take hold, communities are pressing for higher performance at lower cost.

The lion's share of growth in government employment over the past 50 years has not been at the national level, but rather in the ranks of state and local governments. From 1960 to 2007, the number of state and local government workers increased from 6.4 million to more than 16 million. Given those mushrooming numbers, it's easy to understand the parallel growth in physical facilities that took place. At a time of retrenchment, states and communities alike are rethinking their approach to real estate.

The city of San Diego leases more than 500,000 square feet of downtown space—at a cost of $13 million per year. As the city considers whether to renovate or replace the existing city hall, Gensler has shown one clear benefit of consolidating into a new building—it could reduce the city's overall need for office space by 30 percent. Gensler is working closely with the city and its developer to implement a new workplace strategy and standards to meet the city's future program and staff growth.

Gensler's expertise in private-sector workplace projects translates easily to workplace-centric projects in the public realm. The firm's ready access to benchmarking data is one of its unique assets, enabling a public agency to compare its real-estate and space-utilization practices against private-sector companies in its region. This allows local governments to learn from the best practices in the private sector and, ultimately, to attract and retain the most qualified employees.

This is a distinct advantage when it comes to designing for state and local governments. In projects such as the new headquarters for the Port of Long Beach, for example, Gensler is replacing an outdated facility with a fully sustainable office building planned around new ways of working that reflect mobility and the need to collaborate informally, often in small groups. This prototype of the "office building of the future" is designed to enhance personal, organizational, and operational performance. That local government is sponsoring it is of interest; so is the fact that government's new work modes and styles fit well with such sustainability goals as bringing natural light into the interior of the workspace.

State and local governments are increasingly asking for the same high level of building performance that GSA, for example, requires for federal facilities. Yet they also demand true economy of means. Gensler's integrated sustainable design approach focuses on components like structure, foundations, mechanical systems, and cladding and roofing systems to reduce costs and maximize performance.

Government at the community level—whether of a state, a county or region, or a town or city—has the same need for quality, sophistication, and performance in its buildings as government at the national level. The reference points today are wide ranging as public officials look beyond their own borders for precedents. This is not new: ambitious cities have long sought talent wherever they could find it. As a global design firm, Gensler uses its exposure to world cities to share knowledge across all of them.

A growing number of US cities—Chicago, San Francisco, Seattle, and Washington, DC, for example—now require LEED certification for new development over a certain size. Gensler is helping the public agencies charged with enforcing this, and also working with owners and developers to meet both the letter and the spirit of the requirement. In this context, new buildings in the public sector become opportunities to show local communities how best to incorporate sustainable design measures. In China, sustainability is becoming a focal point of the economy, with cities like Shanghai pushing aggressively for innovation in new buildings. Gensler, with two offices in China, is currently designing a super-highrise mixed-use tower in Shanghai that is ground-breaking in its sustainable performance. The city of Shanghai is an investor in the project. Gensler's knowledge of new approaches to sustainable development is already informing its work for public- and private-sector clients elsewhere in the world.

By virtue of their scale and civic importance, civic buildings also play an important part in creating and reinforcing a community's identity. This is a critical dimension of the work Gensler has completed in the government sector. From towns like Snoqualmie, Washington—whose new city hall sets a new tone for a reviving historic center—to regional hubs like San Jose, California—whose international airport has been completely transformed to give Silicon Valley a 21st-century gateway—there is a clear need for public buildings that, among their other attributes, fulfill the aspirations of their communities.

OPPOSITE ●● The modern, sustainable city hall in Snoqualmie, Washington, consolidates public services in a single location, improving their efficiency and delivery in a fast-growing community.

Moscone Convention Center

Moscone West Exhibition Hall
San Francisco, California, USA

In brief

Type: Exhibition building
Completed: 2003
Size: 300,000 sf (exhibit space)
Height: 3 stories
Green factor: Daylighting

Since 1981, Moscone Convention Center has been an important catalyst for investment in the city's South of Market (SoMa) district. To remain competitive, the city and county of San Francisco have been adept at making strategic improvements to the facility over nearly three decades. Gensler has played the lead role in all the additions. In 1991, the firm completed the Esplanade Ballroom, an above-ground plenary area with new meeting space and offices all constructed on top of the original convention center. In 1992, the center opened Moscone North, a massive 520,000-square-foot addition constructed underground. Gensler's newest addition, Moscone West, features a striking three-story glass lobby and such scale-giving devices as multistory bay windows and street-level retail space. This civic building enlivens the SoMa streetscape while making Moscone an even greater business success.

OPPOSITE •• The transparent lobby and interior balconies let convention-goers and passersby engage each other in a spontaneous visual dialogue, reviving Fourth Street as a lively and walkable corridor. **OVERLEAF** •• The building is a prominent landmark in San Francisco's Yerba Buena Center.

Gensler has been involved with Moscone Convention Center's expansion since 1986, when it began the work of doubling the size of the original Moscone Center, adding well over half a million square feet. The design team proposed to do this in two phases in order to keep the center in operation. Phase I added the Esplanade Ballroom building, including a 43,000-square-foot ballroom, a 14,000-square-foot lobby usable as prefunction space, additional meeting rooms, and administrative offices. The project resolved vertical circulation problems in the original building and improved its kitchen and banquet facilities. Phase II produced Moscone North, connected to the original convention center by an underground concourse beneath Howard Street. This 198,000-square-foot addition features daylit exhibition spaces. Its seven-foot-thick foundation is designed to withstand constant groundwater pressure, while its roof supports the overhead load of Yerba Buena Center's cultural facilities and landscaped park.

The latest addition, Moscone West, is a 300,000-square-foot, standalone exposition building that extends the convention center westward across Fourth Street. Designed in joint venture with Michael Willis Architects and Kwan Henmi Architecture, Moscone West responds to its urban context and the steady flow of pedestrian traffic. An expansive lobby gives the center a welcoming presence and, at the prominent corner of Fourth and Howard, opens onto a broad entry plaza where the façade steps back from the sidewalk. The building creates a visual dialogue between convention-goers and passersby on the street. Its transparency and brightly illuminated presence in the evening make it a welcome and activating presence along Fourth Street, the main pedestrian route from Moscone Center to regional transit along Market Street and to the hotels, stores, and restaurants on and around Union Square.

Moscone West's sweeping, transparent façade yields a daylight-filled building, with a 112-foot-tall curtain wall in the prefunction space forming one of California's tallest unsupported glass structures. Flexibility was the key directive for the design of the interior. More than 5,000 linear feet of movable, ceiling-hung panels on the upper two levels allows configurations of up to 19 meeting rooms per floor. The top level also is designed as a large ballroom that can accommodate more than 7,000 people. Generous floor-to-floor heights make Moscone West suitable for trade exhibits of every type.

OPPOSITE ●● Daylight from the full-height curtain wall, one of the tallest unsupported-glass structures in California, fills the triple-floor lobbies.

Design fact

The curtain wall in the prefunction space is one of California's tallest at a height of

112 ft

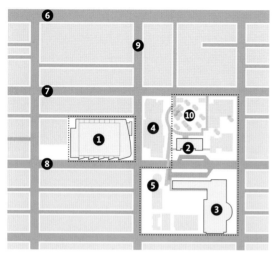

0   200   400   800 ft

BELOW •• Moscone West expands by 45% the convention center's conference and trade show capacity. Its extraordinary flexibility allows separate events to be hosted simultaneously on all three floors.
OPPOSITE, TOP •• A grand canopy along Fourth Street welcomes conventioneers arriving from the hotel and shopping areas around Market Street to the north.
OPPOSITE, BOTTOM •• The upper floors wrap around the building's southeast corner, extending out above the sidewalk to form a protective canopy for the Howard Street entrance.

1: Moscone West
2: Moscone Center North
3: Moscone Center South/Ballroom
4: Metreon
5: Zeum/Carousel
6: Market Street
7: Mission Street
8: Howard Street
9: Fourth Street
10: Esplanade

Level-3 floor plan

1: Configurable exhibition space
2: Exit stairs
3: Movable wall pockets
4: Telecom, electrical, and AV controls
5: Monumental stairway
6: Passenger elevators
7: Balcony
8: Escalator
9: Open to below
10: Freight elevators
11: Bay window
12: HVAC shaft
13: Pantry
14: Service corridor
15: Restrooms

OPPOSITE, TOP •• Movable panels on the upper two levels allow configurations of up to 19 meeting rooms per floor. OPPOSITE, BOTTOM •• Level 3 doubles as a large ballroom that can accommodate some of the city's biggest events. OVERLEAF •• From outside, the window wall makes Moscone West appear as a multilevel stage set—humming with activity by day, a calm, light-filled lantern by night.

Exhibition configuration

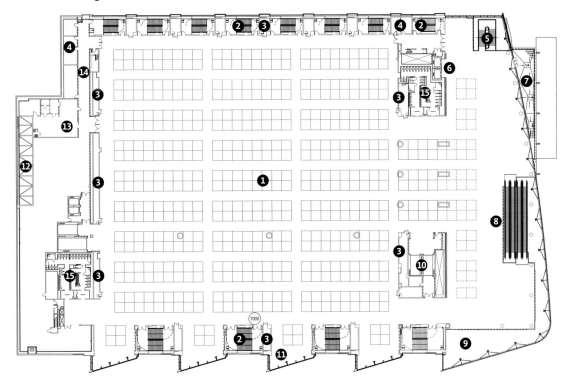

Meeting configuration

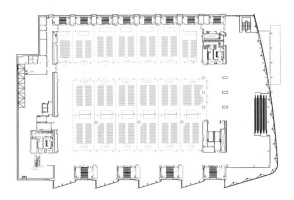

Plenary configuration

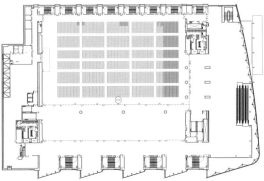

Port of Long Beach

Headquarters Office Building
Long Beach, California, USA

In brief

Type: Office building
Completion: 2013
Size: 265,000 sf
Height: 9 stories
LEED registered, targeting Platinum

Founded in 1911 at the mouth of the Los Angeles River, the Port of Long Beach is one of the world's busiest seaports. After decades of growth, the Port decided to expand its headquarters complex. Gensler is designing a new office building that the Port envisions as an icon on the waterfront. Rising prominently along Queensway Bay, the long, narrow building consists of two wings that join at a series of stacked, two-story atriums. Framing a forecourt at the plaza level is a low pavilion housing a public boardroom. A "smart skin" and an expansive photovoltaic array are among the sustainable design strategies the building incorporates. Narrower depths and an offset core maximize daylight to the office floors. These features define a new level of performance for public-sector office buildings.

OPPOSITE •• The headquarters rests on top of a parking garage that forms a podium for the building and provides the foundation for an entry plaza and elevated garden.

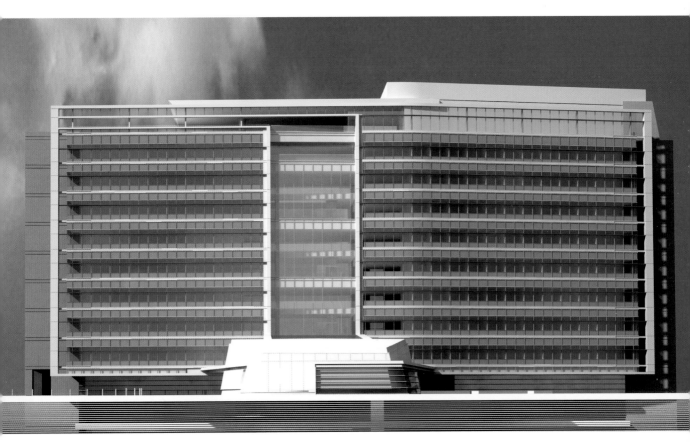

After several expansions over the past nine decades, the Port's original 800 acres had grown to encompass 7,600 acres of wharves, cargo terminals, roadways, rail yards, and shipping channels. The existing administration building, completed in the late 1950s, lacked the seismic safety and technological sophistication to remain viable in the 21st century. Gensler proposed a new combined facility on a 17-acre site near the existing administration building. The resulting nine-story headquarters office building is designed as a waterfront icon, the broad sweep of its south-facing elevation affording panoramic views of the port. (The project is in design, with many alternatives still in consideration.)

Each pair of floors shares a communal atrium, which is centrally located to encourage informal meetings and collaboration among internal departments. When viewed from the outside, clear glazing in the atriums will give the impression of a void slicing through the middle of the building, forming a symbolic portal from the port into the city. On the first floor, a spacious, glass-enclosed prefunction area extends from the lobby and bridges between the office building and a new 220-seat boardroom located adjacent to a circular drop-off area. This provides separate access for people attending meetings of the Port's Board of Harbor Commissioners. The building sits on a podium-like two-level parking structure. Drivers enter from the sides to park or make their way up a ramp from the west side, past an amphitheater, and arrive at the building's main entrance. Covering much of the 470-car parking structure is a green roof that provides additional surface for landscaped gardens.

The building's orientation and configuration maximize its energy performance, with solid stair cores on the ends that partially shade the east and west façades from sun exposure. The "smart skin" on the south façade incorporates insulated glass, horizontal sun shades, fritted glass at the atriums, and reflective louvers within the clerestory windows that bounce daylight into the 65- to 75-foot-deep office floors. Under-floor air distribution with raised-access flooring and demountable partitions provides added flexibility. The building will use recycled and locally manufactured materials, as well as thermal energy storage and integral photovoltaic cells to increase its environmental performance.

OPPOSITE, TOP •• The "smart skin" combines insulated glass, horizontal sun shades, fritted glass (atriums), and light-reflecting louvers (clerestory windows). **OPPOSITE, BOTTOM** •• The 220-seat boardroom is separated from the tower for better access and security.

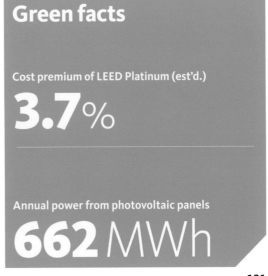

Green facts

Cost premium of LEED Platinum (est'd.)

3.7%

Annual power from photovoltaic panels

662 MWh

1: Office building
2: Boardroom building
3: Maintenance yard
4: Visitor parking
5: Service entrance
6: Employee parking entrance
7: Public entrance
8: Loading dock/trash
9: Maintenance building
10: Outdoor dining
11: Photovoltaic array (above)
12: Covered vehicle storage
13: Central plant
14: Emergency fire department access
15: Public drop-off
16: Bicycle storage

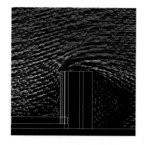

ABOVE AND OPPOSITE •• Exhaustive fluid dynamics studies were conducted to investigate the viability of wind power on the tower. Before the option was ruled out, the design team explored the architectural implications of incorporating wind turbines on the façade. **OVERLEAF** •• The new office building embodies the port's commitment to reducing its environmental impact.

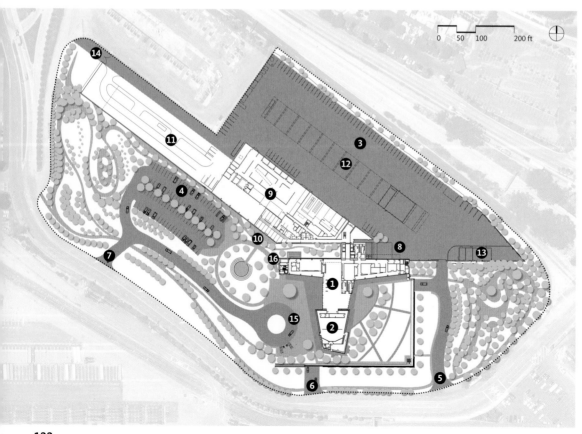

RIGHT ∘∘ The light-filled café on the ground level enjoys direct views to the public garden terrace. OPPOSITE, TOP ∘∘ A building cross-section shows how the design creates double-height atriums on every other floor. OPPOSITE, BOTTOM ∘∘ The adjacency of elevators, stairs, pantries, and meeting spaces makes the atriums natural places for chance meetings and collaboration.

Floor plans

1: Demountable office partition
2: Atrium
3: Atrium bridge
4: Interconnecting stair
5: Lantern wall
6: Conference room

Lower level

Upper level

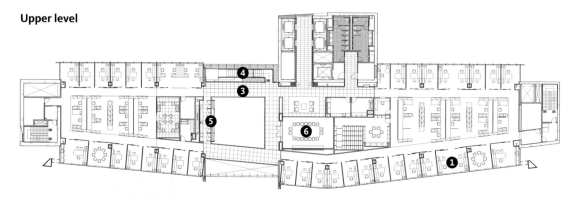

Mineta San Jose International Airport

North Concourse, Terminal B
San Jose, California, USA

In brief

Type: Airside concourse
Completed: 2009
Size: 380,000 sf
Height: 3 stories
LEED NC registered

Long overdue for a new facility, the city of San Jose has embarked on the complete remaking of Mineta San Jose International Airport, recognizing its role as Silicon Valley's gateway. Gensler's new master plan uses the full potential of the airport's tightly packed site—hemmed in by two freeways, the Guadalupe River, and existing development. The modernization program includes a new central terminal, a consolidated parking facility, and an improved roadway system—led off by the Gensler-designed North Concourse (with Steinberg Architects). The 1,600-foot-long building uses new forms and materials to achieve a dynamic appearance that embodies the innovative spirit of Silicon Valley.

OPPOSITE •• The concourse's curved, translucent roof, draped with a mesh-like shade fabric, recalls the canvas sunscreens that protect Latin American street markets. OVERLEAF •• The dynamic façade of the 1,600-foot-long concourse exploits digital design tools and fabrication methods.

Gensler created a master plan for Mineta San Jose International Airport's modernization using a collaborative and inclusive community workshop–based planning process. The design team posited a range of potential users. With names and personalities, these "avatars" helped show how the airport would be experienced by passengers, neighbors, staff, and others. This resulted in strong community backing for the plan, and clear design direction for its components.

The North Concourse's undulating façade is inspired by the imagery associated with San Jose's long and close association with Silicon Valley. From the double-helix of the design team's original concept, the building developed into a potent symbol of high-tech/biotech innovation. Fittingly, three-dimensional design software was used to create elements like the asymmetrical roof form that hovers over sail-like, perforated aluminum screens, which appear to peel away from the building's core.

Founded by the Spanish, San Jose still has a *paseo*, a five-block market street that links a variety of uses downtown to create a regional destination. Gensler applied the same idea to the concourse. Instead of fabric placed over market stalls, the curved, translucent roof of the linear promenade is shaded with draped panels of mesh-like fabric. With departing passengers spending more time on the airside, the promenade offers 29,000 square feet of shops, cafés, and restaurants. For scale and ease of use, stopping points with restrooms are provided every 300 feet, designed to a hospitality standard of quality and finish.

A commitment to limit the airport's environmental impact greatly influenced the design of the new concourse and its operating systems. Interior daylight is provided by the skylights and a full-height glass façade with integral light shelves facing the airfield. Digital controls balance light fixtures and natural light to reduce energy use. Further energy gains are realized using a low-velocity displacement ventilation system in the public areas. The shape of the building complements the performance of the ventilation system by allowing hot air to stratify in the high ceiling area and be vented to the outside.

Site plan

0   300 600   1200 ft

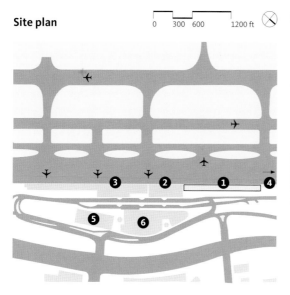

1: North Concourse
2: Terminal B, Phase 1
3: Terminal B, Phase 2
4: Terminal A
5: Parking garage
6: CONRAC

OPPOSITE •• Changes in sun angle make the façade appear perforated or solid. BELOW •• Three-dimensional concept studies helped the design team generate the terminal's form. BOTTOM •• The airport's modernization adds a central terminal, a parking garage, a consolidated rental car facility (CONRAC), and an improved roadway.

OPPOSITE •• The concourse expands the airport's capacity with 10 new gates and 29,000 square feet of retail space. OVERLEAF •• Augmenting the illumination from the roof structure, full-height glass facing the airfield provides additional natural light and views of the hills surrounding Silicon Valley.

Green facts

Energy savings vs. California Title 24	Water savings vs. conventional
14%	**20%**

Landside elevation

1: Perforated aluminum
2: Staggered insulated metal panels with integrated lights
3: Blue aluminum/glass plate
4: Plaster base
5: Insulated metal "outer skin"
6: Perforated aluminum brise soleil façade

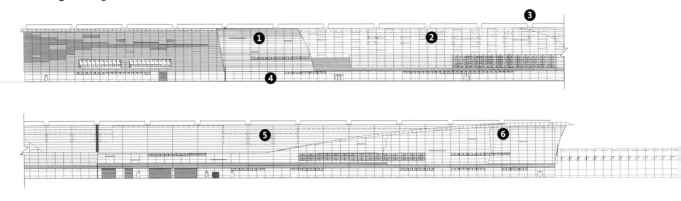

Typical section

1: Mechanical
2: Skylight
3: Boarding area
4: Light mast
5: Fixed bridge
6: Ground service area/ equipment
7: Operations
8: Utility/baggage
9: Retail/concessions
10: Insulated metal
11: Profile metal

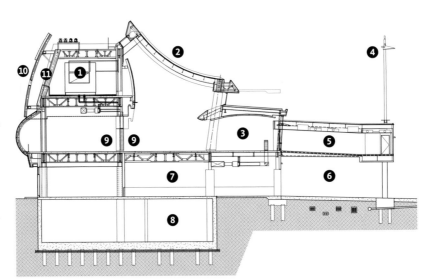

134

Chicago Transit Authority

Dan Ryan Red Line Improvements
Chicago, Illinois, USA

In brief

Type: Transit station renovations
Completed: 2006
Number of stations: 7
Number of bridges: 2
Green factor: Renovation

Built in the mid-1960s along the Dan Ryan Expressway, the passenger stations on Chicago's Red Line hold a special place in the pantheon of the city's architecture. Minimalist and function-driven, they were originally designed by Myron Goldsmith, a Chicago modernist whose structural expressionism was leavened by sensitive detailing. After four decades of hard use, the platforms were cluttered, the walls were damaged and discolored, and the roofs were leaking badly. The Chicago Transit Authority (CTA) asked Gensler to upgrade the appearance and functionality of seven stations from 35th to 87th streets. As part of a comprehensive renovation, Gensler rebuilt the stations, improved circulation and wayfinding, upgraded utility connections, and enhanced connections with the city's bus line.

OPPOSITE •• Broad entrance canopies were added at the street level, providing generous shelter for transferring bus passengers negotiating Chicago's brutal winters. **OVERLEAF ••** Inspired by the design of the original stations at track level, the sweeping, street-level canopies overhang the bridges like giant trellises.

Gensler approached the project as an exercise in historic preservation, stripping the stations back to their painted steel frames and replacing the fabric to its original appearance. Of particular interest are the translucent polycarbonate domes, whose mid-century modern character is fundamental to Goldsmith's design. Gensler searched widely before locating a company in Maine that could reproduce them. The station walls were reconstructed, along with upgrades such as new flooring, enhanced lighting, customer-assistance kiosks, and seating with integral storage for sand and salt.

An important project goal was to improve linkages within the CTA system, so the designers paid great attention to connections between bus and train routes. Broad entrance canopies were added at the street level, providing generous shelter for bus passengers negotiating Chicago's winter snowstorms or summer squalls. Made from a grid of narrow steel members painted white, a respectful nod to Goldsmith's station design, the sweeping canopies overhang the bridges like giant trellises.

The upgrading of the Sox/35th Street Station included the bridge crossing the Dan Ryan Expressway. The busy station serves US Cellular Field, home of the Chicago White Sox baseball team, on one side of the bridge, and the Illinois Institute of Technology campus on the other. The bridge also links two neighborhoods that were separated by 14 lanes of traffic when the expressway was first built. Gensler added new windbreaks to make the bridge crossing safer and easier. They also recast the bridge as a plaza on game days—a place where hawkers sell baseball paraphernalia and fans meet and greet. The bridge is embellished along its span with large steel lettering identifying the White Sox and IIT. (Ross Barney + Jankowski served as architect of record for the 35th Street Bridge.)

While the seven-station renovation program was being carried out, utility infrastructure was upgraded to improve power reliability and delivery to the Red Line stations. Two new electrical substations and a variety of upgrades to existing substations and equipment were accomplished in the midst of Illinois's busiest expressway without closing any stations or disrupting either traffic or train service.

Chicago transit map

1:	Chinatown/Cermak	6:	69th Street
2:	Sox/35th Street	7:	79th Street
3:	47th Street	8:	87th Street
4:	Garfield	9:	Downtown Chicago
5:	63rd Street		

OPPOSITE •• Unsightly chain-link fencing along the 35th Street Bridge was replaced with canted, exposed steel canopies on each side of the span.

Section of pedestrian canopy

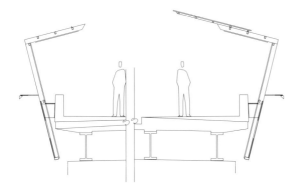

Sox/35th Street Station plan

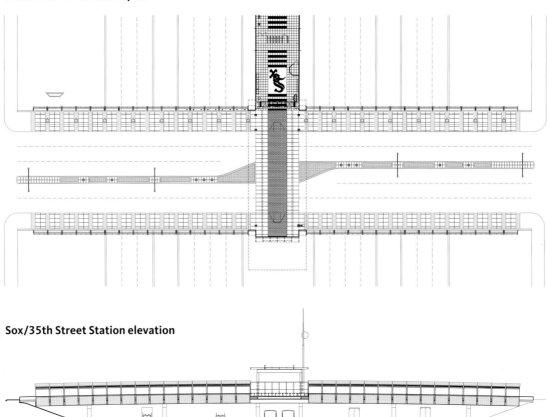

Sox/35th Street Station elevation

Snoqualmie City Hall

Snoqualmie, Washington, USA

The city of Snoqualmie was an important logging town in the late 19th century. In the 20th, it was best known as a tourist stopping point on the way to Snoqualmie Falls. In the 21st, its location 30 miles east of Seattle has made it a desirable residential community within that larger city's orbit. Explosive growth left the historic town center wanting for attention. To help revitalize the area and encourage private investment, Snoqualmie invited Gensler to design a new administration building in the heart of town. The new Snoqualmie City Hall consolidates public services that were scattered in five different places, improving their efficiency and delivery. Modern and sustainable, it shows developers what's possible in the city.

OPPOSITE •• **Modern and sustainable, the new city hall has improved the efficiency and delivery of public services to residents of Snoqualmie.**
OVERLEAF •• **Angled walls and gradations of gray coloring reflect the rugged cliffs of Mount Si.**

Gensler's design team began its work by exploring the characteristics that make Snoqualmie unique. Not far outside the city are the foothills of the Cascade Mountains, dominated by towering Mount Si. The city also boasts an 1890 train depot remaining from Snoqualmie's days as a transportation hub. Contextual cues provided by the powerful natural surroundings and wood construction of the depot inspired the city hall's form and materials. A large shed roof sheltering the city hall, for example, recalls traditional roof forms that are part of the town's architectural heritage. The roof captures rainwater and, using scuppers, lets it spill out over the rockery as a seasonal water feature.

Landscaped mounds and a stone-lined, planted swale distinguish the new public plaza, a gathering space tucked against the west side of the building. Tall vertical panels set at varying angles conceal the building's service functions while echoing the rugged form of Mount Si, which rises in the background. In scale and character, the east façade responds to the context of Maple Avenue, a main route through town. Along this face of the building, the regular pattern of canopies and exterior doors anticipates potential conversion of the ground floor to retail space—a clear sign of the city's belief in the viability of its downtown and an eventual exit strategy for a growing city that expects to outgrow the building.

A generous public lobby leads to the council chambers, which are configured so they can be used for after-hours community events, while the rest of the building is secured. Because of their high occupancy, the chambers are the only area of the building with a conventional HVAC system—radiant heating and cooling are used elsewhere. Operable windows let staff adjust air flow for their own comfort. Air temperature is monitored and maintained automatically by a system that opens and closes the dampers in the large shafts that exhaust warm air from the building. These measures reduce energy use by 30 percent.

OPPOSITE, TOP AND BOTTOM •• **The light-filled public lobby leads to the first-floor council chambers, while providing convenient access to departmental offices on both floors of the building.**

Green fact

Energy savings vs. conventional

30%

Site plan and level-1 floor plan

1: Garden
2: Main entrance
3: Lobby
4: Reception

5: Council chambers
6: Open offices
7: Lunchroom
8: Offices

ABOVE, LEFT •• Light shelves increase daylight and reduce heat gain. ABOVE, RIGHT •• Rain scuppers create a natural water feature. OPPOSITE •• The west façade overlooks an informally landscaped garden. OVERLEAF •• The cedar-clad east façade reflects the town's character.

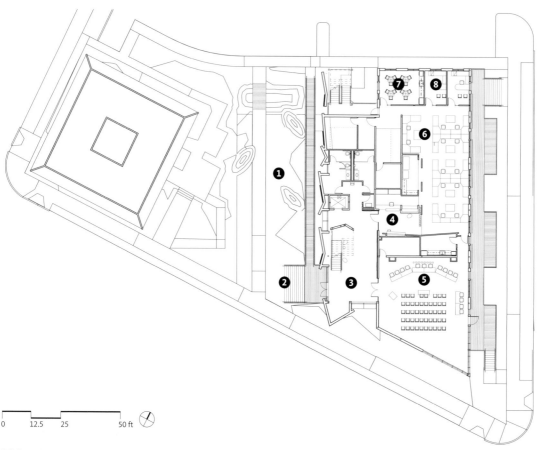

0   12.5   25   50 ft

Los Angeles Police Department

Memorial to Fallen Officers
Los Angeles, California, USA

In brief

Type: Memorial
Completed: 2009
Length: 32 ft
Height: 13 ft

The Los Angeles Police Department's Memorial to Fallen Officers pays moving tribute to those who have died in the line of duty. Prominently sited in the plaza adjacent to the new police headquarters, the memorial is located in downtown Los Angeles, across 1st Street from City Hall. This wall formed of illuminated brass plates is the focal point of a public space shared by the police and the community they are sworn to protect. A glimmering symbol of the department as a whole and the individuals who comprise it, the memorial also speaks to the human price of upholding the rule of law and ensuring public safety in a highly diverse metropolis. To create a suitable public memorial for 21st-century Los Angeles, Gensler designed it as "a work of many hands" that continues to engage the community.

OPPOSITE ●● The names of fallen officers come into clear view as people draw close to the Memorial to Fallen Officers. OVERLEAF ●● From a distance, the memorial appears as a solid wall of illuminated brass.

159

Context plan   0   150   300   600 ft

1: Memorial
2: LAPD Headquarters
3: City Hall
4: St. Vibiana's
5: Caltrans Building

6: Los Angeles Street
7: Main Street
8: Spring Street
9: 1st Street
10: 2nd Street

OPPOSITE •• Situated on the plaza to the east of the new headquarters of the Los Angeles Police Department, the memorial reveals itself as a textured composition of more than 2,000 individual brass nameplates.

The Los Angeles Police Department Memorial to Fallen Officers was organized by Gensler as a pro bono design project, in response to a request from the Los Angeles Police Foundation board. The foundation specified the memorial's location—a public plaza at the LAPD headquarters—and asked that it be sufficiently transparent that no one could ever hide behind it and threaten the police. Designers in Gensler's Los Angeles office began by exploring the nature and meaning of a public memorial in the city, and how this might apply to the Los Angeles Police Department project. Thirty different schemes were initially generated through a collaborative charrette process, in which the designs were reviewed and discussed and winnowed down to the most promising concepts.

The design combines four essential elements—site, wall, badge, and light—in a tight composition that integrates the memorial with the plaza surrounding it. The north side of the plaza is an active civic space, a formal setting for police ceremonies. The south side features an informal garden, a quieter, contemplative place. The memorial mediates between these two spaces, a symbol of the preferred role of the police as mediators in the community, enforcing the law in a humane and empathetic way. After debating the most appropriate material for the memorial, the design team settled on the brass badge, the traditional symbol of agency and authority for police departments around the world.

To bring the concept into reality, Gensler employed a completely digital design and delivery process that supported the seamless collaboration among the geographically distributed team members responsible for designing, fabricating, and installing the memorial. The memorial is made up of more than 2,000 brass plates that reflect and refract daylight to create a shimmering presence. From a distance, the memorial appears as a solid, glowing surface. Closer up, it proves to be an assemblage of discrete, suspended plates, some already engraved with the names of the fallen—a place of memory, mourning, and rededication, emblematic of the LAPD's service to the community.

ABOVE •• While the memorial honors individuals who died in the line of duty, it also symbolizes the police department as a whole. OPPOSITE •• More than 200 fallen officers have been memorialized.

BELOW •• The 32-foot-long memorial occupies a prominent spot in the new public plaza. The north side of the plaza (a) is an active civic space, while the south side (b) contains a contemplative garden.

Axonometric

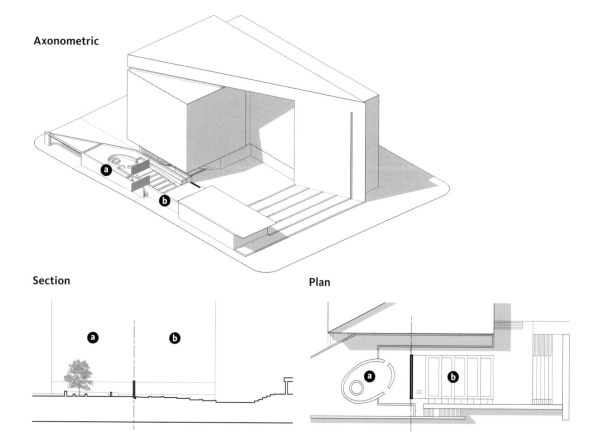

Section

Plan

ABIEL BARRON
DETECTIVE – 03/25/2003
GENE TILFORD NASH
SERGEANT – 10/20/1958
ROGER R. WARREN JR.
POLICEMAN – 05/08/1967
WADSWORTH
PAGLIOTTI

Index

Image credits

All images are credited to Gensler unless otherwise noted.

Benjamin Benschneider: page 105; page 148; pages 150-151; page 152, both; page 154, top left and top right; page 155; pages 156-157

Carillion: page 40; page 43, both

Crown Copyright: page ii, right; page 36; pages 38-39; page 41, both; page 42; page 44, both; page 45, inside back cover, left

Dennis Gilbert: page 75; page 76; page 77, both; page 80; page 81, top

Ryan Gobuty/Gensler: inside front cover, right; page 11; page 159, pages 160-161; page 162; page 164, top left and top right; page 165

David Goddard/Getty Images News/Getty Images: page 37

Roland Halbe: page 106; pages 108-109; page 110; page 112, bottom right, page 113, both, page 114, top; pages 116-117; back cover

Steve Hall/Hedrich Blessing: page 139; pages 140-141; page 143; page 144, both; pages 146-147

Tom Kessler: front cover; page 8; page 26; pages 28-29; page 30; page 31, both; page 33, bottom right; pages 34-35

Michelle Litvin: page 95; page 96; page 97, all; page 100, all; page 101

Blake Mourer/Gensler: page 15; page 66; page 67; page 68, all; page 71; pages 72-73

Prakash Patel: inside front cover, left; page 4; page 17; pages 18-19; page 21; page 22, both; pages 24-25

Frank Pinkers: page ii, left; page 46; pages 48-49; page 50, top; pages 56-57

Owen Raggett/Gensler: page 79

Sherman Takata: page i, right; page 112, bottom left; page 114, bottom; page 128; pages 130-131; page 132, both; pages 136-137; inside back cover, right

Tanenaka Corporation: page 7; page 51, middle and bottom; page 52; page 53

Paul Warchol: page 58; page 59; pages 60-61; page 62, both; page 65